AMORY LOVINS: Pool, Afon Cwm-llan

A'm gwlad gynefin   *And my native country*
Yw bro sêr hefin.   *Is the home of summer stars.*

                                   —TALIESIN (6TH C.)

I must go up again and hear the song:

[5

. . . white brooks swift singing lovely, chanting trees,

and, where the green can thrust no further, strong
from seas of rock an older tune than these.

AMORY LOVINS: *On Glyder Fawr, storm*

Where water stands in arching walls like stone
and stone has flowed like water whirling clear
upon the land in flood I must be gone
to bring my brittle ashen harp-frame there.

The song of towers is within: and I
shall string my tautened harp with ice and snow
and granite, tuning it to chords of sky,
and palest winds shall pluck it when they blow:
the faintly sounding cry of silver strings
will lure me on with dream of silent wings.

I look down
Upon the world,
Spread below me
In the setting sun.

Out of the shadowy forest
Winds the road
by which I came,
Deserted.

Even as I gaze,
A bank of cloud
Sweeps down,
And, at a stroke,
Blots out the world.

But far above me,
In the sun's last rays
Still gleams
The topmost peak.

Liu Tzu Hui (1101-1147)

Eryri, the Mountains of Longing

by Amory Lovins
with photographs by Philip Evans

introduction by Sir Charles Evans
edited, with a foreword, by David R. Brower

FRIENDS OF THE EARTH ◯ SAN FRANCISCO, NEW YORK, LONDON, PARIS

The McCall Publishing Company, New York   *George Allen and Unwin Ltd, London*

Acknowledgement

This book could not have grown from dream to substance without the help of so many people that it would be a book in itself to name them all; indeed, many of the most essential contributors never told me their names. But I must try to thank some in particular to whom no amount of thanks could repay my debt, and hope that the fact and intention of this book will at least make the rest feel that their kindness has borne fruit.

Philip Howell Evans, friend and photographer, patiently taught me how to make photographs. For that gift—the art of seeing and the craft of reducing my circles of confusion—I owe him far too much to say.

My companions in the Oxford University and the Oxford Mountaineering Clubs have shown me their gardens in Eryri, and in time have come along to look at mine; for a thousand moments clear in my mind I am grateful to them all, and to the fellow-wanderers met by chance who have shared with me their knowledge of country that only a handful of people know intimately.

The scholarship of Professor Idris L. Foster has saved me from many errors of translation and orthography in the place-names, though I have doubtless added new mistakes in their stead. Anthony Conran's repeated hospitality, both domestic and literary, has contributed some of the best of the quotations that complement the photographs. And several kind Welshmen, especially Meic Haines, have helped to introduce me to the Old Language and other treasures of the Cymry.

I am indebted to the authors and publishers who have let me quote from their works, and particularly to R. S. Thomas, who, when I wrote to ask him if I could use two of his poems, very kindly sent me a third ("The River"), which is published here for the first time. Further enriching our image of Eryri are the photographs graciously contributed by Evan Roberts, Elizabeth Phipps, John Cleare, Ian G. Crook, and Dr. J. K. St. Joseph. The water-colour painting facing the Foreword appears through the courtesy of its owner, Mr. Eric W. Phipps.

Let me also thank any copyright holders who, despite our efforts, we have been unable to trace because we were borrowing from the research of others—secondhand discoveries, we confess, but no less moving.

The largest section of the text surveys the very complex problems of the Snowdonia National Park, an endangered reserve of which Eryri is an important part. Dr. R. Elfyn Hughes and many of his expert colleagues at the Nature Conservancy (Bangor) aided my research by providing scientific information on conservation problems in the Park. I thank especially Dr. Tom Pritchard, Iorwerth Ellis-Williams, Evan Roberts, John Gittins, Leo Taylor, Warren Martin, Brian Ducker, and Dr. Alan Buse. Equally essential help in many forms, direct and indirect, came from G. Rhys Edwards, Mrs. Cecily Williams-Ellis, Professor P. W. Richards, Dr. William Lacey, C. J. Tuck, Peter Hoy, John Barton, David Blunt, Jon Tinker, Edwin Matthews, and Graham Searle. But I must make clear that although many of the facts in the text are borrowed, the opinions are all mine and my responsibility.

Many people will recognize in the text the improvements they suggested. Some of the most valuable criticisms came from my parents, Miriam and Gerald Lovins, and my sister, Julie Beth Lovins, who did not let an ocean and a postal strike get in the way of their encouragement.

Friends of the Earth saw what this book could be and then made it so: David Brower in particular had the persistent faith to turn idea into execution and the consistent skill to lead faith to fulfillment, aided by the daily miracles of Karl De Schutter's photo-engravers in Antwerp (especially of Louis Cooremans). Believing W. H. Murray's testament of what moves from the springs of commitment, and watching it all come true, David and Philip and I have come to suspect that some special power has been lent us by the spirit, the hwyl, of Eryri. If I have made some of this hwyl live on paper, it is the doing of the courteous and hospitable people of Eryri—the shepherds and farmers who have shared with me their stories and songs and, on occasion, their homes. To these people, who gave me so freely of their love of the land, this book is dedicated.

A.B.L.

We are grateful for permission to reproduce this copyright material:

W. H. Murray, OBE and J. M. Dent and Sons Ltd. (London): four excerpts from *Mountaineering in Scotland* (1947, rev. ed. 1962, paperback 1966).

Anthony Conran and Penguin Books Ltd. (Harmondsworth, Middlesex): five excerpts from *The Penguin Book of Welsh Verse* (1967).

Anthony Conran: the poem "Pre-Cambrian" and excerpts from the poems "Open Sesame" and "The Marsh," all from *Collected Poems*, Gee and Son, Denbigh, Vol. 2 (1965) and Vol. 3 (1966).

James Morris and the Editor of the *Alpine Journal*: an excerpt from "Climbing from the Outside," *Alp. J.* May 1964.

Reynold A. Nicholson and George Allen and Unwin Ltd. (London): an excerpt from the poem "Universal Love," from *Rumi* (1950).

R. S. Thomas and Rupert Hart-Davis (Granada Publishing Ltd., London): the poems "The Moor" (from *Pietà*, 1966) and "The Small Window" (from *Not That He Brought Flowers*, 1968).

R. S. Thomas: the unpublished poem "The River."

J. M. Dent and Sons Ltd. (London), New Directions Publishing Corporation (New York), and the Trustees for the Copyrights of the late Dylan Thomas: an excerpt from the poem "Fern Hill," from Dylan Thomas, *Collected Poems*. Copyright 1946 by New Directions Publishing Corporation. Reprinted by permission of New Directions Publishing Corporation and of J. M. Dent and Sons Ltd.

Gaston Rébuffat, B. Arthaud, and Kaye and Ward Ltd. (London): an excerpt from *Between Heaven and Earth* by Gaston Rébuffat. Original French text © B. Arthaud 1969. English text © Nicholas Vane (Publishers) Ltd. 1965 by permission of Kaye and Ward Ltd. Translated by Eleanor Brockett.

Col. Laurens van der Post, The Hogarth Press Ltd. (London), and William Morrow and Co. Inc. (New York) for an excerpt from *The Heart of the Hunter*.

The Estate of Robert Frost, Edward Connery Lathem, Jonathan Cape Ltd. (London), and Holt, Rinehart and Winston, Inc. (New York): an excerpt from the poem "Desert Places" from *The Poetry of Robert Frost*, edited by Edward Connery Lathem. Copyright 1936 by Robert Frost. Copyright © 1964 by Lesley Frost Ballantine. Copyright © 1969 by Holt, Rinehart and Winston, Inc. Reprinted by permission of Holt, Rinehart and Winson, Inc. and of Jonathan Cape Ltd.

George Allen and Unwin Ltd. (London) and Houghton Mifflin Co. (Boston): an excerpt from *The Lord of the Rings* (Vol. 2, *The Fellowship of the Ring*) by J. R. R. Tolkien.

Hughes a'i Fab, Cyhoeddwyr, Wrecsam: an excerpt from the poem "Argoed," from *Caniadau*, by Thomas Gwynn Jones (1970, first published 1934).

Faber and Faber Ltd. (London): the poem "The Secret Springs" by Michael Roberts, reprinted by permission of Faber and Faber Ltd. from *Collected Poems*.

Evan Roberts, Elizabeth A. R. Phipps, John Cleare, and Ian G. Crook for permission to reproduce their photographs, copyright in which is reserved to the respective photographers; Dr. J. K. St. Joseph, copyright in whose aerial photograph (from the Cambridge University Collection) is reserved to Cambridge University; Eric W. Phipps, owner of the John Varley watercolour painting.

Albert Einstein, William Sloane Associates (New York), an excerpt from *The Universe and Dr. Einstein*, by Lincoln Barnett, © 1950.

Aldo Leopold, Oxford University Press, Inc. (New York), excerpts from *A Sand County Almanac, and Sketches from Here and There*, by Aldo Leopold, © 1949.

Joseph Wood Krutch, William Sloane Associates (New York), excerpts from *The Voice of the Desert*, by Joseph Wood Krutch, © 1956, and *Grand Canyon*, by Joseph Wood Krutch, © 1957, 1958.

John Muir, Houghton Mifflin Company (Boston), excerpts from *My First Summer in the Sierra*, by John Muir, © 1911 by John Muir; © 1939 by Wanda Muir Hannah.

Loren Eiseley, Atheneum Publishers (New York), an excerpt from *The Firmament of Time*, by Loren Eiseley, © 1960; Random House, Inc. (New York), an excerpt from *The Immense Journey*, by Loren Eiseley, © 1957; Harper & Row (New York), an excerpt from *The Mind As Nature*, by Loren Eiseley, © 1962.

Paul Brooks, *The Atlantic Monthly* (Boston), an excerpt from "The Pressure of Numbers," by Paul Brooks, © 1961.

University of California Press (Berkeley), *The Hundred Names: A Short Introduction to the Study of Chinese Poetry, with Illustrative Translations*, by Henry H. Hart, the poem, "Halfway up the Mountain," by Liu Tzu Hui, translation © 1933 by the Regents of the University of California.

The near landscape is valuable and lovable because of its nearness,
not something to be disregarded and shrugged off; it is where children are reared
and what they take away in their minds to their long future.
What ground could be more hallowed?

SIR FRANK FRASER DARLING

Contents

SIXTY-FOUR COLOUR PLATES

Foreword

Civilizations are buried in the graveyards of their own mistakes
but as each died of its greed, its carelessness, or its effeteness
another took its place. That was because civilizations took their character
from a locality or a region. Today, ours is a global civilization.
It is not bounded by the Tigris and the Euphrates. It is the whole world.
. . . It is a community so interdependent that every mistake we make
is exaggerated on a world-scale.—LORD RITCHIE-CALDER

SANTAYANA tells us that those who cannot remember history are condemned to repeat it. Lord Ritchie-Calder, in his address to The Conservation Society in 1968, suggests one reason why history is not so helpful as it was. There are more reasons why, for this exploding time, there is no remembered history to guide us. A history that tucks atoms safely away in a Periodic Table can tell us nothing about how to control an Atomic Pestilence, the ultimate flowering of the Technological Epidemic. A history that dwells on one people's petty thefts from another cannot prepare us to deal with the grand larceny of this generation's attack on the Earth's biological capital—an inheritance intended to serve an untold number of generations of mankind and of other living things.

History cannot help us handle Now because there was never in history a Now like this one. The recent doubling of gross national product has assaulted the environment as never before—and the next doubling is in the making in a chain-letter madness that besets us. Those who object hear strident, emotional calls for Calm and Moderation by those who profit from apathy and postponement of the day of reckoning, who do not understand, as René Dubos does, that trend is not destiny.

In the United States, environmental concern has been intense—and so alas, as Paul Ehrlich reports, has been an ecological backlash. In one attempt to reverse the backlash, Friends of the Earth are publishing *Eryri*, and hope that the beauty of it, will bring a timely question back into the forefront of the minds of the intelligent lay public and the leaders they influence: What, at long last, should we do about what is happening to the earth? Each citizen hoping to be responsible, whatever his flag, can help find an answer. The question arises from man-made problems; men and women can solve them—once they realize that there will be no UK, US, USSR, China, Japan, or anyone on a dead planet. All nations, the US in the lead in an unhappy race, have been killing it, treating this planet as if we had a spare one, as if nature were our enemy. We lack the perspective that comes from placing man's experience in context with the Earth's.

For example, if we compare the six days of creation in Genesis with the four thousand million years of the earth's age, all day Monday and half of Tuesday is just a construction project. At Tuesday noon a living cell appears and undergoes mitosis. All the rest of Tuesday and Wednesday, Thursday and Friday, and well into Saturday, life expands and becomes more diverse, more stable, more beautiful. At four o'clock on the afternoon of Saturday, the last day of creation, the age of reptiles comes on-stage; at nine o'clock it goes off stage. Just before the age of reptiles ends, there are redwoods—and just before redwoods, the pelican (a 90-million-year-old life form now threatened with extinction by DDT and man's urge to usurp the Earth). At three minutes before midnight, man appears. One quarter of a second before midnight, a bearded man, anti-establishment, talking of peace and brotherhood, and Christianity is on the planet.

Then, one-fortieth of a second before midnight, enters the industrial revolution. It is midnight now, and who will propose that we slow it down? So far, growth-and-pollution-addicted nations have been asking for still more speed. Overdeveloped, underdeveloped, and normal nations alike believe that some kind of technological magic will stretch a finite earth. There is no such magic. Technology accelerates the liberation of resources, yes, but it is not creating them; it is finding and moving and using them up, then looking for the energy to repeat the process with progressively poorer materials, moving them faster, making them into smaller, less recoverable fragments for a diminishing proportion of the earth's growing masses of people. Wisely used, technology should enable us to do more with less, but the change to such use has barely begun. We have not yet learned to ask, before undertaking a vast project, What does it cost the earth?

One thing it costs is wildness; and wildness itself, we are just perceiving, holds answers to questions man has not yet learned how to ask. In obliterating wilderness, the physicist J. H. Rush points out, man repudiates the evolutionary force that put him on this planet and in a deeply terrifying sense is on his own. By merely letting our present momentum sweep us on with it, we can grind through the world's last wild places swiftly. Just the undisciplined dash for energy sources can by itself obliterate wilderness. Eventually the sources will be gone—the damsites, the fossil fuels, the places to isolate atomic waste if we ever find them—so we will learn to use less energy, not more; to live within the earth's income instead of exploding and spilling our way through capital the earth took thousands of millions of years to acquire.

The insistent question remains: Do we return to ways the earth can sustain while the earth still has wildness in it, or do we postpone the inevitable turning until we have severed outright and irrevocably those unbroken living connections to the beginning of life that wilderness has preserved? Dare we repudiate the evolutionary force?

Better goals are desirable, worth predicting now, worth the struggle to make the predictions come true, far superior to acquiescence in forecasts we have been getting lately of a world devoid first of charm, then of love, and finally of life.

Eryri, The Mountains of Longing, is the first title in the series, The Earth's Wild Places, to deal with a country that has so little wildness left. Sir Frank Fraser Darling speaks of 250,000 acres of dereliction in Britain and points out, in the 1969 Reith Lectures, that those acres "are just the bare bones of our degradation; the more subtle effects of air and water pollution have not been presented in any national balance sheet but they are dreadful in the real meaning of that word. Their acreage is far greater." And wildness the rarer.

We hope that what Amory Lovins and Philip Evans say so well in this interpretation, case study, and illustration, reinforced with a chorus of voices arguing for wild places, will bring a new stirring, in Britain and elsewhere, of love for the British earth, will slow the spread of dereliction, and will instead let the virtue of amelioration be substituted for mistakes, so that a land ethic can be exaggerated on a world-scale in the global civilization of which we are all part.

DAVID R. BROWER, *President*
Friends of the Earth, Inc.

San Francisco, California
July 23, 1971

Introduction

MR. LOVINS'S sensitive and appreciative description of Snowdonia is evocative, and his frank declaration of opinion about the dangers which threaten the Park's very existence demands thought. He writes both of the Park's natural beauty as it is now and of the movements, as he sees them, which put the Park in jeopardy. His description of what we as a nation possess, and his exposition of how that possession might be lost, must command the attention of all who are concerned to preserve for future generations what is left of the Snowdonia we know.

Many of the men and women who live in a predominantly industrial urban society such as ours need access from time to time to what is called a natural environment, to what Mr. Lovins calls wildness. Only by having such access can they maintain that balance and individuality of outlook which upholds their dignity as human beings. In Britain today there is very little wild country to be found but efforts have been made to preserve the pitifully small remnants of Britain's natural beauty in the various National Parks. The Snowdonia National Park, of which Eryri is a rough mountainous corner, is very small and very close to large industrial centres of population, but because it is so clearly wild country, and because it is unique in character in the southern part of these islands, it has a special value: a much travelled New Zealander, who had previously scoffed at my enthusiasm, once said to me after seeing Snowdonia, "I understand now what you mean: you must preserve it at all costs."

I spent much of my early life in or on the edge of the Snowdonia Park, and I live there now. In thirty or forty years I have actually seen many of the changes described by Mr. Lovins, changes at first slow and barely perceptible, in recent years swifter and much more obvious.

I have seen Snowdonia change from a fastness of moor and mountain, ill supplied with roads, and empty of all but the shepherd, the naturalist, and the occasional sportsman and mountain walker or climber, to a land which only reveals its old magic charm under the worst conditions of weather, a land traversed by roads which are made wider and more straight each year, and scarred by the tracks of many feet. Such wildness and traces of its natural state as remain are being constantly eroded on a small scale by individual self-interest, and on a large scale by the demands of national and commercial interests; they are eroded also, sad to say, by the massive uncontrolled invasion of those who truly love the mountains but whose presence, without some restraint, destroys the very thing they need and seek. Britain is a small and crowded country: we cannot enjoy, for the sake of our pockets, unbridled technological and commercial exploitation of our countryside and at the same time enjoy, for the sake of our souls, unrestricted access to limitless wild country.

It is high time for us in Britain to decide as a nation on the proper balance between what is good for the pocket and what is good for the soul and to act deliberately to preserve that balance; we must not leave the outcome to chance or to the pressure of events which may take place quietly and produce unnoticed situations which compromise the future of our Parks. It is equally important to ensure that means are found to enforce the consequences of whatever decision is made. If we decide to have National Parks we must state clearly where they are, what they are to be and what is not permitted there, and we must legislate to ensure that they are inviolate.

Other countries have done this. In Britain, because we have less space, the problem is more difficult to resolve; and for the same reason it is more urgent.

It is of the first importance to us and to our children that we recognize the special quality of Eryri and understand the contribution made by wild country to man's spiritual well-being. We must wake up now to the dangers which may beset this small but uniquely wild and mountainous corner of Wales.

Bangor, Arfon
4 April 1971

CHARLES EVANS

Preface

WHEN I first came to study in Britain in 1967, I decided to travel there before visiting the Continent, lest I never get around to seeing what was close to home. By a lucky chance, the first place I went was Eryri, and I have hardly gone anywhere else since. It is that sort of place. Eryri is only a small corner of a small peninsula of a small island, but going there is like falling into a very deep well of memory and solitude. Once you are in Eryri, every other paradise seems somehow paler and less important than before. You are immersed in the singing of mountains and sea, and you cannot get out again. The shepherd who spoke to me of "mynydd-oedd yn llawn hiraeth," mountains full of longing, meant that the land feels a sorrow for things gone, but longing is also what you feel whenever you are somewhere else.

This book is the story of the rocks and sky and water and living things in a tiny island of wildness. It is so small an island that a man could walk across it in a day. The web of its life is tenuous, stretched nearly to breaking-point by the conversion of its dense forests to barren grazing-moors. Year-round roads perforate its fastnesses, hordes trample its fragile grass, jets rip its clouds, builders nibble at its valleys, engineers covet its lakes, miners lust after its metals. Yet by some ancient virtue, the land still has the elusive and vivid flavour of all wild places. I do not know if it can stay wild much longer, for it is too small and delicate to have the ecological inertia to defend itself against the automobile, and too few people have discovered the luminous beauty that suave mining companies now want to defile. The people of Britain desire the automobile and the mine, and that is all right, but it does not make a full life. I hope to persuade them to value just as highly what Eryri offers them, and not to spend it too quickly. The task of this book is to show how much poorer we would all be if, for lack of caring, we let this bit of wildness slip away, to be exploited into producing for our alleged benefit all the things that do not matter.

On memorials from an age more poetic than ours, I have seen the epitaph *Sit eo terræ levis*, Let the earth rest lightly on him. I hope the epitaph of mankind will not be *Non erat terrae levis*, He did not rest lightly on the earth. The planet that has borne us, and that would forever bear us lightly if we had the normal good manners of a guest, has begun to groan beneath our feet. We should remember that boorish guests are seldom asked back. To treat the earth with respect and kindness, we must belong to the land that belongs to us; and to discover how we may enter into the life of the land, we must go back and seek our own roots, in a place where we still have some hope of finding them—in living land, in wildness.

It may be misleading to talk of "wild places for their own sake": what we really want is wild places for our sake—to teach us harmony, and a humility that we are apt to forget in a world of prestressed concrete. Yet to benefit from a wild place that we have conserved, we need not even see it, let alone toy with and thus corrupt it. It is enough to know it is there and we love it. The beginning of that knowledge can come from this book; but the love must come from you. Love, as David Brower has remarked, is a nonextinguishable resource: the more we bestow, the more we have left. There is now so little land in which we can find peace that we must save all we can, so that there will always be a place to feel whole, places to remind us that we were born into a community. This we must do because we love the earth, and because we love our children.

AMORY BLOCH LOVINS

Merton College, Oxford
Dydd Gŵyl Ddewi (1 March) 1971

Photographers' Note

I F WE HAD a lifetime in which to photograph Eryri, and if (which is not likely enough) Eryri stayed as beautiful as it now is for that long, we could still only hint at its photographic possibilities. In the half-year's full-time photography we have each done [during eight years for P.H.E. and three for A.B.L.], we have only been able to whistle the tune, not sing the full chorus. We would also have liked to photograph more to the south, in the Moelwyn and Hebog ranges and on into Meirion; for Eryri, while it is the highest of the mountain-groups of Wales, is just one of many. The trouble with such extension is that there is no end to it; so we have merely gazed, longingly, at the peaks outside northern Gwynedd, whose southern boundary we have set near Beddgelert.

Eryri's lighting is its glory and the photographer's despair. Light, not the camera, is the tool of the photographer, and the light of Eryri is the very unusual result of high latitude, the Gulf Stream, maritime climate on a windward coast, steep topography, and volcanic rock, all combined as nowhere else (except perhaps in the Isle of Skye). But the best of Eryri's light comes to him who waits—and waits—and waits. Mountain photographers who have never worked on the west coast of Britain cannot imagine its splendid opportunities for frustration. If the Sierra is the Range of Light and the Black Cuillin the Range of Mist, Eryri is surely the Range of Flickering. Elsewhere the light may shine for minutes at a time, summoned perhaps by an Ansel Adams's stern command, but we lack that influence, and in Eryri a mere second or two of the right light, darting out like a toad's tongue and then gone, is all we can get.

A man can make, in Eryri, an average of one strong photograph in about a week's climbing if he is alert and lucky; being neither, we have taken more than ten thousand miniature-format frames of colour and then painfully distilled. Much of the distillation has been automatic, on technical grounds, for above the valleys we have often had to choose between technically imperfect pictures and no pictures at all. At times the dim light and the wind (for which my logbook shows a three-year average of about twenty-five miles an hour) have combined to give us both those choices. But when the ridges peep out of dense cloud, when the lens isn't covered with snow, when the gale abates enough so that a hand can be spared for the camera, and when we struggle free from the quagmire that the search for an elusive foreground has led us into, then sometimes the ephemeral light comes to us; certain things start to happen and we have our reward, great beyond telling.

Both because the camera cannot replace the eye and because we have shown only part of a part of Gwynedd, we hope you will be able to go into the land and see it for yourself, and perhaps learn from it a little about where you have come from and where you are going. To us the land has been very generous. It has given us a revelation of unity; never again will we see antithesis in nature (in light and dark, storm and calm, we and it), nor will we impose value-judgements on nature's supposed oppositions, as the townsman does when he curses rain and rejoices in sun. We have also discovered in Eryri a truer sense of perspective, especially in time: the lesson of stability in flow, of poise in the midst of motion, on a scale in which we are so insignificant that we have no word small enough to say it.

Eryri's greatest gift to us has been teaching us how to see. As Rébuffat says, "To be able really to see, it is not enough to open the eyes, one must first open one's heart." The lines sifting and integrating in our viewfinders, the arching parabolas rising out of the earth and returning again, have taken us with them and built us a cathedral. Where before we looked through a window, now the world is within our eyes and we look there. Wherever we go now, we will be in Eryri, which is to us as another land was to Wallace Stegner: "The sky in that country came clear down to the ground on every side, and it was full of great weathers, and clouds, and winds, and hawks." Eryri has taught us what a beautiful planet we live on. In return for that gift of the land, we can think of no better thanks than to try to put it in your eyes too, for between the few men who are trying to protect places like Eryri and the few who are trying to diminish them, there you stand: you and your multitudes, with the power to decide whether a book like this will be a requiem or a beginning.

P.H.E., A.B.L.

These were the mountains of true vision, not of this world,
causing one to mourn his lost splendour during this life of exile,
yet rejoicing him with promise of a return.

—W. H. MURRAY

. . . not the mystery of clearness such as is seen in the Alps and Himalaya, where range after range recedes into the infinite distance, till the white snow peaks cannot be distinguished from the clouds, but . . . the secret beauty born of the mists, the rain, and the sunshine, in a quiet and untroubled land. . . .

—NORMAN COLLIE

I. ERYRI

*There is no corner of Europe that I know which so moves me
with the awe and majesty of great things as does this mass
of the northern Welsh mountains seen from this corner of their silent sea.*
—HILAIRE BELLOC

Mountains

"BUT I'VE JUST COME from America," I explained in halting Welsh. "Only learning the Old Language, I am." The hikers leaned helpless on their staves and laughed to make the wind blow backwards off the ridge. "You can't fool us," they insisted. "We know perfectly well you come from Cardiff, for there is such a barbarous Southern accent with you!"

Then I knew I had come to the northern end of the North.

I stood in the heart of Eryri on a narrow platform in the sky. Underfoot lay the jagged rocks of the Glyder range, dropping away in black cliffs. To the south, across the Pass of Llanberis, the spires of the Snowdon massif sprang into the clouds, and behind lay the final ranges of Eryri and the beginning of Meirion, southern half of the vast Snowdonia National Park. To the west glinted the Irish Sea, to the east the moors of Denbighshire. Under the huge whaleback ridges of the Carneddau, the luminous green ribbon of Nant Ffrancon pointed northwards across the Menai Strait to the Holy Island of Anglesey, fertile Mother of Wales and ancient home of Druids; beyond, the Sea.

In Caernarvonshire, in this far corner of Wales, I saw the three major ranges of Eryri—Snowdon, Glyder, Carneddau— as the core of a rugged valley-riven terrain with such variety in its twenty-mile square that a lifetime would not be enough to learn its ways. Mountains, tarns, torrents, valleys, rivers, moors, forests, islands, lakes, cliffs, screes, marshes, estuaries, quarries, and seacoast all lay within my sight.

Rather than concealing secret valleys in deep clefts between explored ranges, Eryri conceals above her settled valleys the secret mountains known well by very few. On the map, no part of Eryri is more than four miles from a road. In reality, many parts of Eryri might as well be four hundred miles from a road for all the chance you have of meeting anyone there, and there are wild hidden places where nobody has gone within living memory.

It was here that Celtic Britain was most successful in repelling foreign invaders, and here that her last kings ruled; here that Darwin and his contemporaries came to understand glacial action, fossils, and other fundamentals of geology; here that much of British (and hence world) mountaineering was born, and here too that modern climbers have trained for ascents in the world's great ranges; here that the classic studies of arctic-alpine botany were done; near here that the Investiture of the Prince of Wales was recently held in Caernarvon Castle; and equally near here that the legendary Welsh adventurer Madoc set sail westward with a band of colonists who some say may have become the Mandan Indians.

Against the stone of Eryri armies beyond count have broken like water. At Pont-rhyd-goch there used to be an old lady who, if you passed by her window, would have you in to tea, with warm milk fresh from the cow. I asked her one day where the name was from, for it means Bridge of the Red Ford, and it is in Nant y Benglog, the Valley of the Skull, and Welsh place-names have a meaning. She told me how at that spot the

Ordovices swept down from the fastness of Llugwy to ambush the cavalry of Rome; and as she gave a blow-by-blow account of the battle, her years dropped away, unnoticed amid the lapse of nineteen centuries, and such fire was in her that I thought she must have fought the Romans herself. Perhaps she did.

Only a few miles from there lie the barrows, monoliths, stone circles, and forts of Bronze Age and Iron Age man. Time means little in such a place. When the mist comes down over the moors, the sombre stones seem to gather a magic, and I would not be surprised if a gnarled Neolithic man suddenly appeared among them, a shadow among twisting wraiths of smoke, stooping to search for a lost arrowhead.

Later history, too, is likely to appear out of the ground, and may be indistinguishable from legends handed down. Most of the major peaks of Eryri are sacred places of long ago, and over all of them stalks the Brenin Llwyd, the Grey King, who causes mysterious disappearances. The summit of Snowdon itself is said to be the tomb of Rhita Gawr, greatest of the race of giants, who wove his robe from the beards of vanquished kings. Everywhere are traces of the legend of King Arthur and Merlin, and signs of the feats of ancient warriors.

More than once a shepherd, pitying my ignorance, has left his chores to recount these tales, for history is in him as sight is in the eye. "Gwlad beirdd a chantorion, enwogion o fri," sings the National Anthem: Land of poets, singers, and heroes. The Eryri hill-farmer's pasture could cover his ancestors of three or four thousand years ago, his language is at its best in epic narrative or sorrowing lyric, his tradition is more bardic than literary; so it is no wonder that history and legend may mean much the same to him and seem to include him in their flow. Folk memories in Eryri may recall pre-Christian events: there are families who have lived so long in a valley near Snowdon that they claim as ancestors the Fair Folk who put the stars in the sky.

Steep ridges split Eryri's people into isolated valley communities, each worshipping in its own Chapel. "When I was a girl," said the old lady of Pont-rhyd-goch, "eight families we had here, see, and the Chapel full. My brothers and I walked the ridges up by there barefoot, not to have holes in the shoes for Chapel. But many of the boys went off to the cities, to London, or even to America, thinking to have more. Four farms, now, not eight. No preacher with us here since the Old Gentleman died, years ago now, but every Sunday we come to Chapel to hear from the Book and sing the hymns. These things we can still do for ourselves."

Nowhere is the musical Welsh language, far older than English in England, more vigorous than in Caernarvonshire, but regional differences of dialect are especially marked here. I know two villages only a few miles apart over a high ridge, with perceptible differences of pronunciation or inflexion in several words—and with at least one noun that is masculine in one village and feminine in the other. If you go several valleys farther, say ten miles, the accumulated changes amount to a difference of dialect. Modern transportation has not removed these anomalies: the men of the Ogwen Valley have more business with Capel Curig, five miles east, or even with the University city of Bangor, nine miles north, than with Nant Peris, a four-mile walk over (or fifteen-odd miles around) the Glyder ridge.

These differences of speech need not trouble the traveler, since almost everyone in Eryri knows some English, but differences of place-names may cause confusion. The same place may have several different local names, depending on where you view it from—what looks like, and is called, a Blue Cliff on one side may be a Red Dome on the other. Conversely, different places may have a name in common—there are various summits called The Cairn, for example, and several spiny ridges called The Rake. The government maps, adding to the fun, occasionally change or omit popular local names. And a place that somehow gets left out of the name game can still play—you can call it The Peak (or whatever) With No Name, even if the people in the next valley have had their own excellent name for it for centuries.

Because place-names are usually descriptive, some must be long in order to be specific. "The Church by the Upper Farm on the Stream in the Marsh" is a reasonable length—no worse, really, than the English "Burnham-Deepdale-with-Brancaster-Staithe" or "St. Andrew Holborn-above-the-Bars with St. George-the-Martyr"; but the Englishman is sometimes outdone. I once saw a Welsh deed bounded from "the big oak at the cold end of the grove where Rhys the Swamp shot the fox in the year when the Chapel roof leaked."

There is said to be a bridge in North Wales whose name was so long that people started calling it Pont-yr-enw-maith, the Bridge of the Long Name,—and now they've forgotten what the name was! The story, though more easily found than the bridge, seems entirely in character.

But I cannot imagine a Welshman who would call a place by a plain ugly name when he can think of names as beautiful as these: Lake of Longing, Valley of Sound, Cliff of the Wine, Moon Fountain, Wall of Mists, Lake of the Dapple-Grey Mare, Citadel of Light, Silent Moor, Torrent of Clouds, Hill of the Hawk, River Running, Stream That Lies in the Eye of the Sun.

We could enjoy even more of Eryri's place-names if we knew what they all meant. Many of them are too old for that. We are not even certain about "Eryri," although some of the best philologists link the word to the Latin root oriri ('to arise'), yielding instead of 'The Place of Eagles' ('eagle' is eryr) the more prosaic translation 'The Highlands.' The Romans who occupied Wales were never assimilated very well, but many of their words were, and now look deceptively like Romance borrowings.

The specificity of the Welsh place-names adds great richness. Instead of saying simply Mount Such-and-such, you describe in the name exactly what sort of mountain it is—whether it is a pen, moel, mynydd, carn, carnedd, crib, braich, gallt, craig, trum, or something else. Like the Eskimo languages that have many words for various kinds of snow, Welsh has a wide range of subtly different terms for the main feature of the landscape.

In contrast, there are few surnames to go around in Wales, so a neat system of descriptive nicknames has evolved. A man might be called Jones the Chapel (because he lives there), or Hughes, Fertilizer (because he sells it), or Williams, Down (because he lives farther down the valley than Williams, Up), or Thomas the Social Security (because he works for the Ministry), or Morgan, Hiccups (because he has them). A wife would be Mrs. Jones the Chapel, and so forth.

The hardness of pronouncing Welsh has, I think, been much exaggerated, and I will bet that in five minutes you can be doing fine at it, for most of the Welsh letters have the same values as in English, all but one have the same values all the time, and every letter is pronounced. The differences are:

The vowels are pure and have roughly the Continental values:

a   as   *arm*
e   as   p*ear*
i   as   *eve*
o   as   *orb*
u   as   *fee*, but with the back of the tongue raised
y   is usually the same as u if stressed and obscure as f*u*n if not
w   is as f*ood* or b*ook* (i.e., the sound may last for a long or a short time; cwm, a steeply enclosed valley or mountainside hollow, rhymes very approximately with tomb)

As for the consonants:

c   as   *c*at
g   as   *g*ay
s   as   *s*ee
j   as   *j*ump
ch as   lo*ch* (gutteral)
dd as   *th*ere (the soft [voiced] *th*)
th as   *th*in (the hard [unvoiced] *th*)
f   as   *v*alue (v is not a Welsh letter)
ff as   *f*ar
ph as   *f*ar
r   is slightly trilled at the tip of the tongue
si before a vowel is usually as English *sh*

Thus English 'Hoover' in Welsh letters would be Hwfyr; 'shop,' siop; 'farther,' ffarddyr; 'gaily,' geli; 'truthful,' trwthffwl. (These last three words are imaginary.) Stress is normally on the next-to-last syllable, and tiny words (such as y, yr, yn, ei, and fy) are not stressed.

There are only two more things to know. The first is that Welsh uses beginnings as well as endings: the first letter of a word may "mutate" (change) in several ways, depending on how the word is being combined with others; for example, pen ('head') might become ei ben ('his head'), ei phen ('her head'), or fy mhen ('my head'). Second, the sound that is written *ll*: put the tip of your tongue against the roof of your mouth, the left edge of your tongue against your left upper teeth, and blow. The air will come out on the right side between your tongue and teeth. Now say 'long.' If you combine these two sounds, you are saying llong ('ship'). That is not too hard. To be more sporting, try Llangollen!

Now, before you start saying There is a lot of complicated old rubbish, ach y fi,—first let me see you write a practical guide to English pronunciation in a couple of little paragraphs.

While you are trying that, you can delight your tongue with the lilt of these: Gallt y Wenallt, Llyn y Cwn, Carnedd y Fíliast, Bwlch y Moch, Carnedd Dafydd, Castell Cidwm, Penllithrig-y-wrach, Cwm-glas.

When you have felt the magic of Celtic words, it is easier to understand the man I met walking under Snowdon very early one morning. When I wished him good-day, he stared as though I had two heads, scuttled off behind some rocks, and I never saw him again. "Was there a plague with him, now then?" I asked a shepherd later. "O, that would be old Ieuan," he explained, "searching for the words to weave his poem for the Eisteddfod."

It is a marvel that the ancient arts of Eryri survive, for the land is bare and harsh, and does not yield a living without great labour. The life of the Caernarvonshire highlands is sheep-farming—the sheep outnumber the people twenty-five to one—and the shepherd seems to spend more time than is in the day tending sick animals, chasing strays, mending fences, and a thousand other tasks. Yet if you are very lucky, when you pass some remote croft in the evening, you may still hear a man singing to the harp. If you are luckier still, he may be setting formal verses with cynghanedd (strictly governed patterns of alliteration, assonance, and internal rhyming and echoing) in penillion style—that is, improvising the song so that it is intricately interwoven with the harp melody, which follows a completely different tune and metre.

Eryri has always been a centre of the brilliant poetic tradition of Wales—a tradition at least fourteen centuries old that has produced probably the most subtle and complex patterns of versification in the world. Both obeying and enlarging the classical forms, the poet in modern Wales retains much of his ancient status as a moral preacher, social critic, and cultural prophet to whom all pay heed. But there is no elite literary caste; the poet may come from any walk of life at all. This is because rural Wales has practically no class distinctions, for everyone is a farmer or a recent descendant of farmers, and all

To a Poet Met in Cwm Dyli

Grey goblet of clouds
not yet drunk by sun: gulls stitch
the sky together.

Under the mountain
a wanderer searches for
substance of his craft:

not metals or gems
or woods or furs but only
words to weave and bind,

words to cast and carve.
He tilts up flat stones to look
underneath for blind

burrowing earth-words.
He parts each stiff clump of grass
to see if quiet

winds, in carding it,
have left any words there. He
seeks words of white flame

to kindle his tongue,
and supple green fern-words, and
words of still water

to flow into the
shapes of vessels. The sun and
the moon bring him words.

The clouds melt and drip
words on him: cold gulls cry words
into the morning.

therefore share the same ties to the soil and to the Old Language.

The most universal of the Welsh rural arts is conversation, and making a sentence is thought an important matter worth craftsmanship. The humour, and there is always some lurking, is quiet and inward, so dry indeed that if you are from northern New England it will make you feel right at home. ("Have you lived here all your life?" "Not yet." Or another example: "What a fearful gale! Do these ships sink very often?" "Just once.") But if you have done a foolish thing, then be from in front of that terse humour, for a few sentences could wither a cactus. Nobody has disposed of demagogues so efficiently since Gwilym Morgan, in Richard Llewellyn's novel *How Green Was My Valley*, said that they "have tongues a yard long and nothing else inside their heads. All the space will be taken to coil up their tongues."

Nor is there any time for a man who has no time for manners. As I stood one day talking to a shepherd by the roadside, a man drove up, splashed a puddle over us, honked the horn, and shouted, "Does it matter which of these roads I take for Dolgellau?" The shepherd replied, with an emphasis, "Not to me," and turned back to his sheep.

Simply to say Eryri is steep is to miss the point of its steepness. It is true that the land has been hung up by one corner to dry, and all the water is running off; but the mountainous character of the major ranges is greatly out of proportion to their height, which is only a little more than three thousand feet above the sea. There are four main reasons why such hills look and act like real mountains.

First, above the valley floors the slopes are entirely bare, offering the eye no standard of scale: there are only strewn stones and tundra-like grasses and lonely grey lakes. Between the blasting wind and the nibbling sheep, trees cannot survive much above a thousand feet, and most of the old oaks, rowans, ashes, and birches that used to flourish below that level have vanished, along with the ancient eagles.

Second, the weather, despite the moderating effect of the nearby ocean, can be severe, with black frosts and hurricane-force winds. Winter weather may be worse at three thousand feet in Wales than at twelve thousand in the Alps, and is much less predictable.

Third, the topography is exceptionally broken; although the rocks are very old, the grinding glaciers of the last great Ice Age finished melting only about ten thousand years ago, and time has not yet softened their works. The savage amphitheatres gnawed from the mountainsides are still as raw as though finished yesterday, the scratches still plain to see on the rocks, the narrow ice-carved ridges steep and rough—and often the only way to a summit.

Finally, because of the dramatic glaciation, many of the ridges rise so steeply in such a short distance that they give a sense of great height, of floating far above the world. Some summits, such as those of the Snowdon group, are so perfectly shaped that they look at least twice their actual height. With a rock face as with a human face, lines and character are more imposing than size. Yr Wyddfa, seen through sea-mist from three miles away, will probably look more majestic than a mountain five times its height, seen through distance-haze from fifteen miles away. This nobility of outline has misled many visiting Alpine and Himalayan guides into ludicrously exaggerated estimates of the size of the Welsh peaks.

A peculiar result of Eryri's compression of many ranges into a small area is that in the valleys you never have space to stand back at a distance and see the peaks in their true proportions. Indeed, many summits are not visible from below. All you can see is piles of black rock, enormously foreshortened and seeming to lean out over you. It is not until you walk to a place across the valley and half a mile higher that you can see the unsuspected new world hovering above the valleys, with range on range marching to the sea.

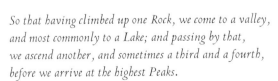

So that having climbed up one Rock, we come to a valley,
and most commonly to a Lake; and passing by that,
we ascend another, and sometimes a third and a fourth,
before we arrive at the highest Peaks.

—EDWARD LHUDY (1695)

Dr. J. K. St. JOSEPH: Aerial view southwest to Yr Wyddfa and Crib Goch/Crib y Ddysgl ridge

This hidden realm seems especially isolated from the everyday world of the motor-tourist (on whose antlike scurryings you can gaze down disdainfully) because high Eryri is as empty and wild as the high Alps—more so, for there are no climbers' huts above the valleys. There are no inhabitants, but only temporary visitors, who come either on foot—mountaineers and, now and then, a naturalist or a photographer—or by air, like the scavenging gulls (or the Royal Air Force mountain-rescue helicopter, which always seems to me a sort of benevolent mechanical vulture). The tourists who take the cog railway up Snowdon, gaze into the mist, and chug down again are the most transient and out-of-place visitors of all. Even the local shepherds need seldom come so high: they can rely on massive dry-stone walls, built with skill to last for centuries, and on the territorial training transmitted by matriarchal old ewes, to hold the ridge-boundaries secure. So although the hill-farmers are natives in the valleys, they too are in a sense trespassers on the high ridges, and are back down the mountain by nightfall.

When I have the chance I love to bivouac overnight on a summit in Eryri and then watch the day opening like a great flower. But there are places where this is seldom done—where the hud, the magic, is inhospitable. By Glyder Fach (Small Heap) is a tower of sharp slates called Castell y Gwynt, the Castle of the Winds, where a tempest can shriek and moan in a terrifying way. They say that the man who spends a wild night there alone will in the morning be either mad or a great poet. I once met an experienced climber who tried it. So strange were the things he heard there that he left before midnight, and ran all the way down to Helyg. He said he was going so fast that he just touched down a foot now and then to steer with; but of what he fled from he would not speak.

Much of Eryri is accessible in summer to the ordinary hiker who does not mind finding his own paths—the maps, guidebooks, and way-markers are often not very helpful. Occasionally there is some awkwardness about trespassing, and wherever there is no marked public footpath you will be wise to ask the landowner's permission. If previous visitors have omitted this basic courtesy, climbed on the dry-stone walls (which loosens them so that they fall down), strewn litter about, trampled the precious pasturage, and left the gates open so that the flocks have strayed, you must not be surprised if the indignant farmer forgets his English, or lets a bull into his lower pasture and puts up a warning sign in Welsh only. (The Welsh for "bull" is tarw—unless it mutates to darw, tharw, or nharw). And once a farmer gives you leave to cross his land, you must take care not to die or disappear on it; that is very bad public relations, as the farmer has enough to do without running search-and-rescue operations for irresponsible foreigners.

There are so many easy routes in Eryri that only one or two of the summits cannot be reached somehow by a steady-headed man (or woman) with hands in pockets. But the special sort of expedition Eryri provides is the day-long scramble, an exhilarating ridge-traverse midway in difficulty between a hike and a rock-climb. Any experienced hill-walker can do a scramble, using hand-holds but (in favourable summer conditions) without any need for a rope. There are half-a-dozen memorable scrambles, among them the Snowdon Horseshoe (Pen-y-pàs, Crib Goch, Crib y Ddysgl, Yr Wyddfa, Lliwedd, Pen-y-pàs), one of the finest one-day circular scrambles in the world.

But for those who do not treat the mountains with due respect, a day's ramble may end unhappily. "There was a man years ago," a shepherd reminisced, "who went to walk high, on a day windy to turn your ears inside-out. I told him what the wind could do, but he was a big man, and proud, and thought he cast two shadows with him, and would not listen. When he was by the Sentinel, the wind took him from there and broke his leg. I saw from below and we went and brought him back. Heavier than a dead parson he was too. Then he told me to think shame, and blamed me for not warning him stronger, if you please. The words were not in my mouth to answer him. In the winter two years after, I heard he had gone to the Black Cliff up by there, and fallen, and now he is looking at the heather, from underneath, indeed, and having more sense, I hope."

The wind in Eryri can blow very hard. I have seen a gust peel off a neat lake-sized slice of water six or eight inches thick from Llyn Idwal, which is about three by eight hundreds of yards, and deposit it intact over some people lunching a quarter-mile away. A wind like that will blow a man fifty feet straight out from a cliff-face at the end of his climbing-rope. If you throw down a rope to rappell on, the wind may blow it right back up to you, inextricably tangled. Sometimes all you can do is lie clutching your ice-axe, the pick imbedded in the ground, and blow around like a weathervane as you listen to the loud flapping of the empty air.

Heavy rain with a Welsh gale behind it will go through almost anything. The squat stone cottages of Eryri have windowless west walls a yard thick, sheathed with inch-thick slates about two feet square; but after a few years the driven rain wears through the slates, which must then be replaced. A farmer I know in the Ogwen Valley had just finished this re-slating last spring when, to his dismay, a freak wind tore the new slates off the house and carried them half a mile up the valley. It was at this same farm that a friend of mine was camping one day when his primus stove was possessed by seven devils, flew straight up into a howling whirlwind, and was never seen again.

Y Gwynt (Detholiad)

Ni'th wŷl drem, noethwal dramawr,
Neu'th glyw mil, nyth y glaw mawr,
Noter wybr natur ebrwydd,
Neitiwr gwiw dros nawtir gwŷdd.

—Dafydd ap Gwilym (*fl.* 1340-70)

The Wind (Excerpt)

Though none see you in your den,
Nest of rains, thousands harken,
Cloud-calligrapher, vaulter
Over nine lands wild and bare.

—translated by Anthony Conran

gnaw of slow grey light
rain spatters the seeking wind
time drips on cold stone

Other dangers of these mountains include stonefall (usually caused by careless people above), avalanches, blizzards, bitter cold, slippery rocks, hail, torrential rain, and the infamous winter whiteout, when you cannot tell the misty sky from the snowy ground, and it is like being inside a ping-pong ball. You can have a rare sort of whiteout without snow, too, when the fog gets thick enough to net salmon in, for then you cannot see as far as your own feet. But all these unusual conditions are predictable and avoidable. The dozen or more climbers and hikers who die each year in Eryri, and the hundreds of lost or injured who keep the volunteer mountain-rescue teams busy, are the victims only of their own carelessness, ignorance, or overconfidence. Many casual hikers, convinced that small mountains are trivial, simply ignore the warnings and pleadings of those who later have to rescue them. But I do not want to discourage good hikers from exploring these mountains; for the competent amateur, Welsh mountaineering is among the safest of active sports.

The only problems I have had while wandering in Eryri have been not dangers but nuisances funny afterwards, like falling into a snow-bridged stream or leaving my lunch within reach of a hungry sheep. A friend of mine, equally unwary of woolly rovers, once neglected to tie up his tent-door securely, and returned from a day's scrambling to find a newborn lamb in his sleeping-bag. I have had a few startling experiences in Eryri, but nothing as dramatic as the novice did who was being taken up through Cwm-glas-bach when the rack-and-pinion locomotive derailed above him on an early test-run on the Snowdon line. As the locomotive hurtled deafeningly past him out of the mist, the novice is said to have remarked, with proper Victorian aplomb, that he was prepared for all sorts of hazards, but hardly for trains falling out of the sky. (I am happy to say that nobody was killed in that incident, and that with anti-derailment devices added, the railway has worked perfectly ever since.)

Eryri has a few morasses. Welsh mud can be something very special, and some of it would mire a flea wearing snow-shoes. Coming down an innocent grassy hillside last year, I was startled to see a violent quaking a few feet to my left. It turned out that a rocky basin full of water, four feet deep and six across, had got covered by a mat of grass indistinguishable from that on solid ground. I had stepped on the very edge of the basin. Fortunately, surprises like that are rare!

It would be kind but wrong not to mention that Eryri is wet. It is first to get the water that the west wind brings from the Sea. How much water depends very much on where you are: annual rainfall is forty or fifty inches in the peripheral valleys, but the summits only a few miles away get some two hundred, at least a trace of which falls on two days in three. (It could be worse; Feste sings in *Twelfth Night* that "the rain it raineth every day.") Eryri's weather changes often and

quickly—a consolation to climbers who are moping in tents and climbing-club huts, or perhaps playing bridge in village pubs and cafés, waiting for the rain to subside to mere fozzle or drinkle. At times they must think they are having not weather but a disease; but they are pessimists, and if they bothered to try it they would find that very few days are too consistently wet for a good scramble.

Some climbs, of course, are best done in the rain. There is a famous route, going up the inside of a huge crack in a cliff, that is supposed to be climbed on a rainy night when you are thoroughly drunk, and it is even better if you are so big that you get stuck halfway up. The darkness and rain don't matter much because you're inside the mountain anyway. It is a safe and easy but peculiarly atmospheric climb—if you can find the beginning of it in a tangled wizard-wood—complete with an upside-down hanging swamp, a gorse-bush that embraces you affectionately, a natural rock arch to bang your head on, a holly-tree you can clutch for dear life, the main ascent up the long chimney (dripping with green slime and negotiated by a motion called "reptation"), and the final emergence like a cork from a bottle (if you aren't too big to pop out) onto an airy perch. Many people, including me, recommend this route as superb, though it is curious that they themselves seldom return for a second ascent.

The heavy rainfall of upland Eryri has its advantages, too, among them the vast array of troutish lakes, streams, rivers, waterfalls, and other apparatus for returning the water to the ocean for re-use. Besides, the steady supply of clouds usually found rolling in from the west, or boiling around Snowdon, or blowing away from here and reappearing there, could not be bettered for drastic changes of lighting, if you will believe your eyes: shafts of sunlight stabbing out of gloom, purple skies with black stripes and green polka-dots, glowing volcanic rock that turns gold or scarlet or bright blue. Sometimes the chameleon-like rock and grass seem to go through all four seasons within an hour.

The shepherds, for all the notice they take of weather and terrain, might as well be hewn from grey stone. Under their feet everything becomes flat and dry, and they seem so much a part of the landscape that you seldom notice them. Much of their work is around the ffridd, the dry-stone-walled pasture or paddock low on the mountainside. In good weather they rarely need to visit their highest land, and the flock is gathered off the tops by men and dogs only twice a year—for shearing or dipping or separating the yearlings (which are sent away to winter on farms with a gentler climate). Every summer, the whole farm household used to move from the lowland hendref to the highland hafod (summer-house) to be nearer the stock, then mostly goats and cows; but this custom has lapsed, and now you will find the stones of the hafod gathering moss in some lonesome cwm no longer visited.

Sheep would often have to be rescued from perilous ledges were there not herds of magnificently horned half-wild goats, released long ago so that with their greater agility they would graze clean the most tempting ledges and keep the sheep from harm. But now and then a greedy sheep must still be brought down with ropes, after being left to weaken so that its kicking will not throw its saviour off-balance. Passing climbers, sometimes enlisted in these impromptu mountain-rescue exercises, are often the first to find the sheep—perhaps sprawled across a belay ledge essential to the safe completion of a route.

These climbing routes, about 1500 of them, crisscross every crag in Eryri. They are described, graded, and classified in section-by-section guidebooks, which treat each route as a series of specified lines (where the climber should go), holds (what supports him), moves (how he gets from one set of holds to the next), and stances (where he pauses to anchor himself to the rock and hold the rope securely while his companion climbs). The modern innovations of route so outnumber the historic classics that the guidebooks are out of date before they can be published. Route-finding competition is very keen, especially among the English "hard men" who swarm into Eryri every weekend.

New routes, judged by highly developed technical and aesthetic criteria, are discovered not only by exploring little-known cliffs and choosing new lines on established ones, but also by "gardening"—pulling off the vegetation concealing rocks in order that they may be climbed on directly. Botanists and National Park Wardens abhor this practice, and with good reason. Many of the plants thus destroyed are precious remnants of the Ice Age flora and will never re-establish themselves. Some are at the southern limit, or even the only site, of their British distribution, and killing them is tearing pages out of botanical history. In past years, the climbers' preference for the acid rocks, which tend to be hard and solid, has protected the plants, most of which grow on the basic rocks. But the recent trend toward climbing on loose cliffs (such as Trigyfylchau, Clogwyn-y-garnedd, and the walls of Cwm-glas-mawr) may prove disastrous for the rare species that have so far escaped the depredations of climbers and sheep. On the north coast and on Anglesey there is a similar conflict of interest between large nesting colonies of sea-birds and large migrant herds of sea-cliff climbers.

The scope of climbing on the already clean rock-faces has expanded enormously since World War II because of the vast increase in the difficulty of what was thought to be climbable. Welsh routes are world-renowned for their great exposure (how far you fall if you come off them), minimal protection (anchorages to the rock to give you something to fall back on and help keep you from falling all the way), and uncommon boldness (requiring confidence that you will not have to rely on the protection). Ingenious new equipment for joining ropes to rocks, much of it invented in Eryri, reduces the risks to an acceptably low level as rock-gymnasts continue to transcend the apparent limits set by friction and gravity, flowing

IAN G. CROOK: Feral goat

EVAN ROBERTS: Saxifraga oppositifolia, Llyn Llydaw

gracefully up walls on which a flake protruding an eighth of an inch may be considered a ledge.

Some of the new equipment has been developed, and nearly all of it is offered for sale, by Joe Brown, a great master of climbing with his own shops in Llanberis and Capel Curig. Only fifteen-odd years ago and a few miles up the back of Snowdon from Llanberis, he transformed the standard of British climbing, in partnership with Don Whillans and other brilliant cragsmen, by "putting up" a series of long, fiercely difficult new routes on Clogwyn Du'r Arddu (Black Precipice of the Black Height)—smooth arching slabs six hundred feet high, curling above a poisonous-looking lake.

Now, hard as the "Cloggy" climbs are, dozens of climbers consider them a playground, and many of the "rock tigers" romp on the sides of the Pass of Llanberis, where the ballet-like ascent of vertical or overhanging walls has become such a spectator sport that at holiday periods it can produce a traffic-jam five miles long. Dinas y Gromlech, Carreg Wastad, Clogwyn y Crochan, Dinas Mot, Y Gurn Las, Y Graig Ddu— these are some of the twenty-odd smooth black walls where enthusiasts (some would say fanatics) climb up, or perhaps fall off, routes with such ominous names as Cenotaph Corner, Cemetery Gates, The Thing, Spectre, Sickle, Grond, Hang-over, The Skull, N'Gombo, The Toad, Surplomb, and Gollum.

Even the language is new to the uninitiated. As I wandered down the Pass one afternoon, a large and furious climber, festooned with hardware, came clanking off the screes and flopped onto a boulder. His clothes were torn, his hands cut, his tight stiff-soled rubber rock-shoes caked in mud; he said things that made the air shudder. I asked him what had happened.

"I was abseiling off a psychological Moac to start a pretty thin pendulum in tension," he explained in a heavy New Zealand accent, "when I heard the chock slipping in the groove, so I quick jammed and slapped in a Troll here and a bong there, and stood up in étriers to have a look. But I felt a great heave from below, and there was some bloody idiot in a cag, Jumaring up one of my abseil lines! Just then my anchor popped, and my fifis tipped, and my runners unzipped, and I came unstuck and bounced feet-first down into a bog."

"What route was that?"

"I'll tell you when it is."

"But what happened to the fool with the prusikers?"

"He faded while I was thrashing in the bog. I threw a crab at him, but it bounced off his hard-hat into the bog and I lost it. Good Chouinard, too. But if I see him I'll hang him from a skyhook with his own slings."

Somewhere in the world there is a climber who should go in fear of his life.

JOHN CLEARE: Peter Crew on the Great Wall, Clogwyn Du'r Arddu

*. . . arwain fi i graig
a fyddo uwch na mi.*
—SALMAU 61:2

*. . . lead Thou me to the rock
that is higher than I.*
—PSALMS 61:2

PHILIP EVANS: Idwal Slabs, start of Charity route

JOHN CLEARE: *Peter Crew on the Girdle Traverse, Carreg Hyll-drem*

The sport of the "hard men" on rock has its counterpart in ice-filled gullies. With ice-axes and crampons, ice-daggers and North Wall hammers, ice-screws and waterproof clothing, the lovers of glistening blue towers and cascading icicles claw their way up near-vertical walls. An especially notorious gully climb is the Devil's Kitchen (Twll Du, or Black Hole), an abrupt gash in the Glyder ridge. It plunges down for hundreds of feet between narrow walls, far above the floor of Cwm Idwal. For protection against the icy waterfalls that thunder down the chasm, some climbers wear a scuba-diver's wet-suit, while others, presumably desiring greater agility, wear nothing at all.

There is a danger that technical virtuosity may smother some of the more traditional and less demanding forms of Welsh mountaineering. It is possible, for example, to traverse the fourteen 3,000-foot peaks of Eryri (thirty miles of rough ground with 9,000 feet of ascent) in less than five-and-a-half hours, for somebody, incredibly, has done so. Knowing that, one may be tempted to dismiss the potential of these mountains for producing lifelong rewards. Nothing could be a greater mistake. Just because some eager technician can climb 900 feet of desperate ice on Clogwyn-y-garnedd, it does not follow that the other routes to Yr Wyddfa are no longer worthwhile. They are on the contrary as beautiful as ever, and can be enjoyed throughout the span of one's life.

Among the finest of the old-fashioned sorts of mountaineering is ordinary hill-walking, and it is at its best on the brilliant days of deep winter, when the snow forms a firm icy crust along the higher slopes. It may then be easier to move about than it is in summer, for the smooth whiteness now covers the jumbled stones; and the main annoyance of summer is removed—that of which H. R. C. Carr wrote feelingly, "Some people carry a waterproof and get wet, while some do not, and get very wet." No, in the cold season the problems are different, and somehow more exciting. The easy scrambles of summer become serious mountaineering ventures, but the limpid clarity of the air shrinks distance until you think you can touch the far ranges, and the mere nine hours of daylight will not matter, for you can see over twenty miles in the moonlight, with ghostly crystalline pinnacles gleaming around you and the breath of the Grey King sighing across the ice.

But whether you cherish the desolate Alpine splendour of Tryfan or the curlews crying over the moor, the brooding boulders of Siabod and Elidir or the ripples in a forest pool, you will find that if you once wander among the mountains of Eryri they will lay a spell on you, and you will never again be able to live far from places that share their solitude.

In the last resort, it is the beauty of the mountain world in the inmost recesses that holds us spellbound, slaves till life ends.

—W. H. Murray

. . . a sparkling halo of gulls—
those birds of inhuman beauty, whose wild eye and stainless plume
seem to me to have been evolved from the world
expressly to embody the true spirit of seaward mountains,
and by their cry, forlornly echoing among the rocks,
to sound the inner music.

—W. H. MURRAY

Gyfnos

Y nos dywell yn distewi, —caddug
Yn cuddio Eryri,
Yr haul yng ngwely'r heli,
A'r lloer yn ariannu'r lli.

—GWALLTER MECHAIN

Nightfall

Silence brought by the dark night: Eryri's
Mountains veiled by mist:
The sun in the bed of brine,
The moon silvering the water.

—translated by ANTHONY CONRAN

Never, in sooth, does the lover seek
  without being sought by his beloved.
When the lightning of love has shot into this heart,
  know that there is love in that heart.
When love of God waxes in thy heart,
  beyond any doubt God has love for thee.
No sound of clapping comes from one hand
  without the other hand.
Divine Wisdom is destiny and decree made us lovers
  of one another.
Because of that fore-ordainment every part of the world
  is paired with its mate.
In the view of the wise, Heaven is man and Earth woman:
  Earth fosters what Heaven lets fall.
When Earth lacks heat, Heaven sends it; when she has lost
  her freshness and moisture, Heaven restores it.
Heaven goes on his rounds, like a husband
  foraging for the wife's sake;
And Earth is busy with housewiferies: she attends to births
  and suckling that which she bears.
Regard Earth and Heaven as endowed with intelligence,
  since they do the work of intelligent beings.
Unless these twain taste pleasure from one another,
  why are they creeping together like sweethearts?
Without the Earth, how should flower and tree blossom?
What, then, would Heaven's water and heat produce?

—RUMI *(translated by* R. A. NICHOLSON)

If there is magic on this planet, it is contained in water. . . .
Once in a lifetime, if one is lucky, one so merges with sunlight and air
and running water that whole eons, the eons that mountains and deserts know,
might pass in a single afternoon without discomfort.
The mind has sunk away into its beginning among old roots
and the obscure tricklings and movings that stir inanimate things.
Like the charmed fairy circle into which a man once stepped,
and upon emergence learned that a whole century had passed
in a single night, one can never quite define this secret;
but it has something to do, I am sure, with common water.
Its substance reaches everywhere; it touches the past and prepares the future;
it moves under the poles and wanders thinly in the heights of air.
It can assume forms of exquisite perfection in a snowflake,
or strip the living to a single shining bone cast up by the sea.

—LOREN EISELEY

Longing

THE SNOW-SQUALL is nearly over now. Just a little northerly shower, it was, the sort that on the ridge might bring hail and the strange lightning that flickers without thunder. But now the last flakes are falling from thinning cloud, and great sullen shafts of sun are scanning the cornices down the valley by Foel Goch. It will be a good crisp afternoon. I know just the place to show you what this low November sun can do. We'll take a stroll onto the Glyder ridge. It should be out of the cloud by the time we get that high.

See there, while you lace your boots, look across at the little crag near the lip of Cwm Llugwy: if the wind catches the fine spindrift just right and whirls it into that warm patch of sunlight by the boulders—if we're lucky—there'll be a rainbow. They often roost just by those rocks. But only for a moment. Did you see it? Already the flash of colour has blinked and vanished. Today it will be even harder than usual to guess where the sunbolts will strike next.

Business now, the silent checklist before we start out. Anorak, mittens, compass, plastic-covered map sections, photographic gear, band to keep spectacles from blowing away. Spare map, compass, food, and socks. Whistle, light rope and cord, foil blanket, first-aid kit, goggles, torch and spare parts, sheath-knife, cagoule, overmitts, extra film, extra extra film, mountain-rescue flares. Altogether less than five pounds in the pack, enough to make it ride well, and occasionally valuable beyond price. Of course one hopes not, but there may come one of those rare moments of professionalism when everything must be done right.

Could you please toss me that down parka? I want to stuff it into the pack too. It must be about freezing and ten knots, so on top it will be about twenty Fahrenheit and thirty knots, too chilly for just anorak and windproof trousers if we want to linger. No crampons today; the snow cannot possibly have consolidated enough since last night, and has no crust beneath. Snowshoes would be more useful if we had any. And we had better put on our waterproof gaiters to seal the space from boots to knees, for the ridge looks plastered up there, floundery and heavily drifted.

No, I won't forget the ice-axe. How can I forget part of my hand? Even when there is no snow lying I tend to carry the axe in Eryri, despite the curious looks it attracts. It is indispensable in gales, for crossing streams in spate, for probing swamps and snow-bridges, for balance and braking on very steep wet grass or scree, as a camera monopod, and on one occasion to discourage a ram that wanted to butt me off the north face of Moel Cynghorion. He had been hand-reared as a lamb, most likely, for lack of a foster ewe, and came to lose all fear of men. Whatever the explanation, I was glad of an axe to brandish. It would have been a long way down.

We could, I suppose, put a few pounds of extra food and gear into the pack and stay the night by Castell y Gwynt; but I don't think tonight is a good time to bivouac. Something odd is going on. Look. The high clouds can't agree with the medium clouds which way to go, and those lens-shaped ones past Pen yr Ole Wen should arouse suspicion. It will be good to get high up so we can look to the north and see what is happening. But at least the cloud is still rising and we have a few hours before anything breaks.

Right, we're off. Let me get the gate. Watch out for the cars along here: they get ten points for each pedestrian. Here, I'll show you the map. See that farm on it? And the long gentle spur running up from behind it at an almost constant grade, all the way to the broad col in the Glyder ridge? There lies our route. Simple topography on the way up, though there are many little branch spurs that diverge as you come down. The spur is broad enough that we can usually drop down onto its east side to get in the lee. There are several steps on the way up, where cold blue pools lie quietly under the wind, but most of the spur is dry and rises just slowly enough to need no effort—if you know how to walk uphill.

That cluster of low grey stone buildings across the cattle-grid and up the little road is our farm, Gwern-y-gof Isaf, the Lower Alders-by-the-Cave. We are in the land, remember, where Gwilym, the son of Meri-Anni and of Jo Bara (Joe Bread, Joe the Baker) can be called Wilmeriannijobara. By that standard, the tenant farmer here gets off lightly with being called Williams Isa', to distinguish him from his brother at the next farm, Gwern-y-gof Uchaf.

Mr. Williams Isa' is one of the few farmers who have official permission for extensive tenting on their land; hence the spatter of mountain tents and the ranks of the Army encampment in the front field. It is a cheerful sight, and probably pays about as well as the thousand-odd sheep. But if we call Mr. Williams Isa' a tenant farmer, it gives the wrong impression of his permanence: his family has held this farm for four centuries and more. Here he is now, working in the complex of mysterious sheds and pens behind the farmhouse, a big weathered man in rubber boots and green oilskins.

He gives us a comprehensive glance from the boots up, judging whether we'll be all right. Aye, he remembers me now from that time I found his ewe cragbound on the headwall last year. I ask him in the language of the country whether we may please go over his land onto the Glyder. A slow smile comes. He must be happy about something. He would be too polite to smile at my accent. "Of course you may. The place for crossing the mountain wall is up by there, and mind the ice at the stream. The first in three months, you are, to ask my permission. You are welcome."

Perhaps we wouldn't be so welcome if we were the two-hundredth party that day to ask his leave; but if things ever get to that state, he'll know what to do. At the moment, he just wants, very reasonably, to know who is tramping through his back-yard, and whether his visitors are likely to kill his cow with a dropped plastic bag or lame his sheep with a discarded tin. I'm not sure I would be so patient in his place. About the tenth time some hiker broke down a wall so my weaning lambs rejoined their mothers, or left a gate open so my rams got onto the mountain too early (thus bringing the lambs in the deadly winter weather before the proper time), or brought a pet poodle into my ffridd in April and panicked the ewes into miscarriages, I think I might do more than just remonstrate. Action first, maybe, and questions afterwards.

Already we are above the level bottom-land and threading our way through the steeper middle part of the farm, the maze of walled meadows that segregate the various kinds of sheep, each in its season, in the intricate pattern that is the essence of hill-farming. And just here is the mountain wall, solid and very old, with a few long stones set into it crossways to serve as a stile. Its roughness, the integrity of the stone, feels good in the hand. Here is about the lowest the snow lies in late autumn and spring, and the highest any substantial trees would grow if the sheep let them. Above here the un-fenced sheepwalk rises uninterrupted to the ridge. The grass is coarse and thin, so poor that an acre will barely support a single sheep if she is hardy. Feel the blades shattering, brittle with frost, beneath our feet; we are carving tracks that will not heal until spring. Let's walk in single file, to trample as little as possible of our host's livelihood. The actual saving of grass is slight, but the idea is not.

You are ten thousand years too late to see the last of the glaciers gouging the cwms out of the north side of the Glyder ridge, but you can easily imagine that the ice down there melted just a few minutes ago, the marks are so new and clear. Our spur, Braich-y-ddeugwm, the Arm of the Two Cwms, gives us a steadily expanding view down into two perfect amphitheatres. That swirling pattern of crags on the walls is like the inside of a clay vessel fresh from the potter's wheel.

Today you should be especially happy that we are on this route, for it is one of the few spurs in Eryri, and the only one from the Glyder to the Ogwen Valley, that is safe whatever the snow conditions may be. The snow is now loose and in-decisive, somewhere between when its fresh branching rays interlock it cohesively and when the grains get welded into a solid block. On a steeper and narrower route than this spur we might be avalanched.

Across the valley you can see another of these gentle spurs, dropping southeasterly from Pen yr Ole Wen, south-westernmost outpost of the Carneddau. Nearly every novice hiker in Eryri has fallen afoul of guidebooks that recommend the direct west-face or southwest-buttress approach. Anyone who can read a contour map, however, knows better. To reach the southeast spur you have to be scrupulous about per-missions. But the spur is safe and very beautiful. It is sur-prisingly out of the wind, it rarely ices, and it never ava-lanches. There are several other spurs in Eryri with the same agreeable properties. I collect them, and the knowledge has served me well. It is a good sort of knowledge to gain in advance.

As you quietly walk up Braich-y-ddeugwm, clearing the stagnant air from the lower storeys of your lungs, be sure you look back. See there, to the north across Nant y Benglog, the old walls of Llugwy. They are fragile tracings on the snow. They recede over the rising moor to the gigantic swelling domes of the Carneddau, the loneliest and wildest of the northern ranges. The great mass of Carnedd Llywelyn bulges high in the distance, usually in cloud. But there it is now; see it while you can. In the wind-blasted mountains radiating from Llywelyn you can find great hidden cliffs, gales and mists that seem almost continuous, and (if you are lucky) a herd of shaggy little ponies, free and swift and elusive. From here the immense landscape of the Carneddau is framed for you on the east by the end of the Glyder range, dropping toward Capel Curig, and on the west by one of the most beautiful mountains in the world.

Tryfan, it is called: a paradigmatic mountain, a mountain you will see in dreams. I can close my eyes and see it at will, every notch and cusp of its silhouette imprinted on my retina from hours of marvelling at it. "This is a rugged, stupendous, and steep high rock," wrote William Williams of Llandegai in 1798, and that is probably what the name means. Tryfan is a thin triangular knife-blade of volcanic rock, set on edge on a slanted sea of grass and boulders. It soars to a three-peaked edge, each summit buttressed by a pillar and the highest summit crowned by two natural obelisks. From the central terrace to the jagged summit-ridge, the walls of the upper East Face sweep aloft, cleanly and very strongly, for nine hundred feet.

In the history of mountaineering, Tryfan is as significant as almost any mountain you can name, both as birthplace and as symbol. When you enter the Ogwen Valley by road from either direction, you round a corner and see Tryfan, and it moves you. It is always the same, yet always different, for more than any other mountain in Eryri it takes on the colour and mood of the light, becoming hundreds of different mountains in one majestic form.

It can also be a menacing mountain; its beauty blinds people to its steepness and iciness. I treat it with great re-spect, for although it is neither technically difficult (by the

. . . Frost enough for crystal building,—glorious fields
of ice-diamonds destined to last but a night.
How lavish is Nature building,
pulling down, creating, destroying,
chasing every material particle from form to form,
ever changing, ever beautiful. . . .

—JOHN MUIR

North Ridge and other scrambling routes) nor objectively dangerous, it is a place where the careless come often to grief, always in the same rather unimaginative ways and always at the worst possible times and places. The same is true of Bristly Ridge, a steep pinnacled arête connecting Bwlch Tryfan, the south col of Tryfan, with Glyder Fach: it is too scrambly and exposed for most novices to feel happy on it, and in the wet or ice it can be insidiously perilous, committing you before you realize it. Reflect on this, and on the silk of the ice on the sharp ridges to the west, as your boots print blue shadows on the snow.

You cannot walk smoothly up Braich-y-ddeugwm on a fair winter afternoon, for the spell of Tryfan keeps breaking your rhythm. No greater mountain has greater character. From this height Tryfan is in its true proportions, not foreshortened. The light is just right now to skim across the upper buttresses and throw them into the greatest relief. The architecture is perfect Gothic, too perfect for man. There is still enough heat from the sun to send showers of powder-snow down from the tops of those gullies; but it is cold enough that the rock pillars themselves glint with metallic verglas. Now, as often, Tryfan is more pleasant to look at than to be at.

Look across at the rock in the sky, and over the col—a glimpse of far peaks, very snowy and framed by luminous mists. Some secret alchemy of light and air gives this place a strange magic. The light is a palpable fluid pervading all things, each partaking according to its quality. For a time, you are granted here a special virtue of seeing, and images bear a vividness of their own. As simple a sight as three reeds thrusting out of the snow can live in the eye with aching clarity.

Already we are up to the final rise of the spur. There are choices here, but this time we shall traverse on the right, to lose as little as possible of the presence of Tryfan. We cannot turn our backs on a queen. Softly now, feel your boots sinking in securely to make the sound steps; Cwm Tryfan gapes below on your right. It is only a minute from here to the col. Ah, we are in luck: the wind has scoured the snow from the frozen lakes, so we are in no danger of walking over them by mistake.

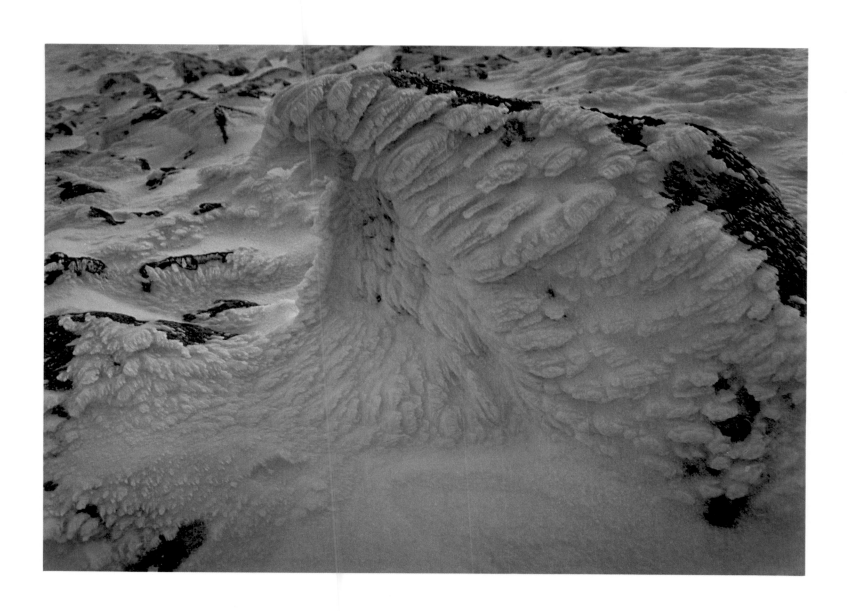

Suddenly, from one step to the next, we are out of shelter into the hiss of white wind, and it has a snarl in it. It brings fast clouds of purple and rich black, riding in a deep and endless Himalayan sky. Here on Bwlch Caseg Fraith, as on all the high cols of Eryri, the wind is funneled into a greater hurry and an uninformative direction. On the saddle, north by east; on the spur, northwest by west; in the sky, north by west; everywhere, keen and searching.

Hop the gullies, miss the little frozen pools, mind the windslab. Let's hurry across the col, chased by the wind, weaving between the seams of the ground, to that far tongue of golden rock set in wind-carved teeth of snow. From the stone sprouts a garden of fresh green icicles, each glimmering as a separate star. Come down here a few yards, and we'll be in the lee for lunch and the southern view.

A few yards down—indeed, yes, you are right to gasp. Never have I found it so clear, even in deep winter. It is never like this except just before or just after a storm. The direct brilliance of the sun skimming across the Tremadoc estuary is so close that we cannot look there. Nant Gwynant is that pool of intense boiling radiance, pure and without colour. The southeast sprawl of snow-capped ranges I have not seen before. They stretch all the way to South Wales. Now you can see how rugged a country is Wales. There is no gentle land in sight, at least not until the Border. Ah, look there on the horizon: the Malverns, it must be; there is nothing else there. Details are sharp at eighty miles. Truly for once we have done something right today. My camera sings its own tune, grasping images that leap out of the snow and printing them on film as they print on my brain. Twenty years hence I am sure these things will be clear in memory.

Something is happening to the weather. Spindrift swishes under the swift low-running sky. A few nibbles of cheese and chocolate and some coffee from the thermos will be all the lunch we have time for, and then we'll have just over an hour before sunset—long enough to spend a few minutes prowling on Glyder Fach, if we don't insist on sunlight to come down by. It looks like a good gamble. In this light there must be something up there. It depends on what the cloud does. Seek and ye shall find.

Lean into the wind, now, and draw up the hood against the sting of spicules. We shall take the direct line to the north rim overlooking Bristly Ridge, whose edge looks viciously iced. We are lucky to have had such an easy ascent. Today we seek mere access, not the technical difficulties that would be easier to find. If we had a rudder and centreboard we could tack right up the summit cone, such is the wind here. In our ears beats the pulsing roar of all high places, the sound of restless sky. Shout or you won't be heard. Watch out for the crevices between the big boulders under the snow, perfect leg-traps if you step in the wrong place. Oof. Don't step where I just stepped. What abominable snow. You may find a modified breast-stroke helpful in the drifts.

Today we must have done two things right, for the Grey King is smiling, and as we break onto the upper ridge he lifts the curtain of cloud from it to expose the towers of the Snowdon group shining to the south. We are looking directly onto the triple summit of the hooded north face of Lliwedd, nearly a thousand feet high, where Arthur's knights sleep sealed in a cave until their King shall return. Ice glitters on the battlements that cross to the steep pyramid of Yr Wyddfa, The Tumulus, the summit and temple of all Wales. From the other side of Yr Wyddfa, cupping a wild roaring hollow, Crib y Ddysgl rears back toward us to link with the extremely narrow ridge Crib Goch, the Red Crest. It parallels Lliwedd across the mile-wide gap of Cwm Dyli, the Valley of Rushing Waters. The cwm is full of summery golden haze, lapping gently at the brim, and the globular sun trembles in it like a ripe apricot; but not with warmth. The backlit ice is sheathing Crib Goch, and a gleaming halo surrounds the silhouette of the underlying pinnacles. Today it would be a beautiful and a terrible place to be, sitting astride the knife-edge with each leg hanging down over an abyss. Crib Goch used to be considered, in summer, the easiest sort of rock-climb, and now is often called only a scramble, but today it would be exacting and ruthless. It looks stark.

And then the sun drops from under a long red cloud, and the light comes onto the Glyder.

O, the light. It is steady now. It pours molten across the ridge, level with the flowing sky, and it lives in each snow-flake and frost-feather. It makes the ice smoke and the rocks rise up with the sound of trumpets. The mountains burn, and yet they are not consumed. The wind dies and there is nothing else in the world, only this.

Only this, and the miracle. These torn stones on which we stand, this blinding fire and the snow on which it casts our shadows high and thin, this freezing air that sears our throats —of these things are we made, and in the grace of an instant and a place we dissolve into them again, single in exaltation. There is no we and no time, nothing but the blazing silent earth. There are no words.

Shivering. That is my body and my blood pumping. I am here, drunk with light. It is intensely cold. We must awake from this wonder, a little, very slowly. Our bodies drag us back. We must put on our down parkas. They rustle loudly and we are clumsy. Still the spell lingers on us and we cannot speak. Mute dwarves, we are, lost in a forest of rock. A huge horizontal slab supported only at one end and the middle, a spray of radiating columns like a frozen fountain of stone, a bouquet of jagged needles sawing at the clouds, and the lunar plateau near the Castle of the Winds: eerie monoliths, silent in worship of the setting sun. Around them all sprays the liquid light, and they are within it and of it, world without end. Dark and supple flow the valleys to the north, for night has fallen in the shadow of the Glyder, and a twist of pale pewter river winks out of the cold fields.

Forty miles beyond, standing out in the Irish Sea, a high black wall seethes, sucking all the light out of that side of the sky. It is a southwest gale, getting visibly taller and nearer. It will be here in force, say force ten, within two hours. The wind has returned to moan in the towers of slate, but already it is backing, so our time of grace is over. We must not linger. The coming of the stars must not find us here. All that matters now is the navigation. This would be no time to get entangled with the crags to the north, or the boulder-fields to the south, or the buttress low on Braich-y-ddeugwm: not at night, with a storm coming.

The shadows now fall long and lonely. The snow has lost its sparkle and become heavy. Slow light settles softer on the earth, all glory faded, and into the sky comes the taste of iron, chill against the teeth.

See, the last glitter: a thin scarlet line on the farthest rim of the ocean in the south. In Eryri the ocean is never far away; here a man can fall under the twin dooms of mountains and sea, he can follow the two passions of solitude, he can be drawn by both the vertical and the horizontal line. Our line, now, is diagonal, and we have several miles to stumble down it, still stunned a little, under the light of a gaunt moon.

The most beautiful and most profound emotion we can experience
is the sensation of the mystical. . . . He to whom this emotion is a stranger,
who can no longer wonder and stand rapt in awe, is as good as dead.
To know that what is impenetrable to us really exists,
manifesting itself as the highest wisdom and the most radiant beauty
which our dull faculties can comprehend only in their most primitive forms—
this knowledge, this feeling is at the center of true religiousness.

—ALBERT EINSTEIN

Bivouac (*c. 1900*)

. . . In joyous bivouacs as in sad ones, on those which preceded victory
as in those which followed defeat, there was always the same fascination . . .
a secret thrill, a sense of wonder, an expectation of something indefinable,
something mysterious that was about to become manifest. . . .
I began to hear a confused murmur of voices and of sounds that came
from every side, rising from the valleys and falling from the summit;
starting from afar, it increased in intensity as it drew nearer,
and then rolled swiftly away in the distance.
It was like the sighs of spirits flying above my head.
Amid the low yet powerful sounds of the huge chorus
I could sometimes distinguish a sharper note, as of anger or lamentation,
which soon ceased, while another voice was uplifted in answer from afar.

   This was the high dialogue between the mountains and the sky,
but on that night all the voices, great and small, seemed to seek out
the tiny mortal who lay lonely and abandoned on the mountain's bosom,
and to relate to him a long and wonderful tale,
as ancient as the world itself.

—GUIDO REY (in *Peaks and Precipices*)

Nature is full of genius, full of the divinity;

so that not a snowflake escapes its fashioning hand. . . .

The same law that shapes the earth-star shapes the snow-star.

As surely as the petals of a flower are fixed,

each of these countless snow-stars comes whirling to earth,

pronouncing thus, with emphasis, the number six. . . .

He takes up the waters of the sea in His hand, leaving the salt;

He disperses it in mist through the skies; He recollects and sprinkles it

like grain in six-rayed snowy stars over the earth,

there to lie till He dissolves its bonds again.

—THOREAU

One may fancy the clouds themselves are plants,
springing up in the skyfields at the call of the sun,
growing in beauty until they reach their prime,
scattering rain and hail like berries and seeds,
then wilting and dying.

Where are the raindrops now? . . .
In winged vapor rising some are already hastening back to the sky,
some have gone into the plants,
creeping through invisible doors into the round rooms of cells,
some are locked in crystals of ice, some in rock crystals,
some in porous moraines to keep their small springs flowing,
some have gone journeying on in the rivers
to join the larger raindrop of the ocean.
From form to form, beauty to beauty,
ever changing, never resting.

—JOHN MUIR

PHILIP EVANS: Reeds, Clogwyn Llechwedd-llô, Cwm-brwynog

Un genhedlaeth a a ymaith, a chenhedlaeth arall a ddaw:
    ond y ddaear a saif byth.
Yr haul hefyd a gyfyd, a'r haul a fachlud, ac a brysura
    i'w le lle y mae yn codi.
Y gwynt a a i'r deau, ac a amgylcha i'r gogledd: y mae
    yn myned oddi amgylch yn wastadol, y mae y gwynt
    yn dychwelyd yn ei gwmpasoedd.
Yr holl afonydd a redant i'r mor, eto nid yw y mor yn
    llawn: o'r lle y daeth yr afonydd, yno y dychwelant
    eilwaith.

                                    —Pregethwr 1:4-7

One generation passeth away, and another generation cometh:
    but the earth abideth forever.
The sun also ariseth, and the sun goeth down, and hasteth
    to his place where he arose.
The wind goeth toward the south, and turneth about
    into the north; it whirleth about continually,
    and the wind returneth again according to his circuits.
All the rivers run into the sea; yet the sea is not full;
    unto the place from whence the rivers come,
    hither they return again.

                                    —Ecclesiastes 1:4-7

. . . And underground streams carry you down
Sapphired, infinite passageways
Ferned and fired of the sparkled ponds . . .
—ANTHONY CONRAN

AMORY LOVINS: Detail, stream with green algae, Cwm-glas-mawr

II. SNOWDONIA NATIONAL PARK

History teaches us that men and nations behave wisely
once they have exhausted all other alternatives. —ABBA EVEN

The Lord giveth, and the Lord taketh away,
but He is no longer the only one to do so. —ALDO LEOPOLD

The wicked flee where no man pursueth,
but they make better time when some one is after them. —CHARLES R. PARKHURST

We [U.S. National Parks] have no money;
we can do no harm. —NEWTON DRURY

1. Roots

THE SNOWDONIA NATIONAL PARK, second largest in Britain, sprawls across 845 square miles of three counties. Its savage northern section, Eryri, and its less harsh southern section, Meirion, together coincide very nearly with the impregnable ancient realm of Gwynedd—"the strongest country within this isle," Sir John Price called it four centuries ago. Because of its outstanding beauty and variety, this diamond-shaped area of riven mountain-blocks was set aside in 1951 as a National Park to be preserved forever for the enjoyment of the nation.

But far from lasting forever, it may not last for a generation. Far from being consecrated for national enjoyment, it is likely to be devastated for private profit. Far from remaining a national pleasure, it may become a national disgrace. These are strong words; yet I fear they are no exaggeration. Plain to see for those who will look are signs that the Park is in grave danger.

How can a National Park protected by an Act of Parliament be despoiled? The answer is simple. Between proposal and passage, the Act was so thoroughly emasculated that the protection it gives the Park is more a concept than a reality.

"Establishing" a National Park in Britain is largely a formality, comparable to drawing a green line on a map, and produces something very different from a National Park in, say, the United States. The Snowdonia National Park is neither national nor a park, for nearly all of it is owned by private interests and operated for private gain, generally in ways unrelated to recreation. You may not go where you like or do what you like in the Park, for you are not on public property. Over this private land, it is true, reigns special administrative machinery that makes it more difficult for the landowner to do what he likes; but no land in Britain is truly inviolate, and the land of the Park, while not devoid of protection, lacks the full measure of protection that it needs to survive.

Five threats, singly or together, could kill the Park within the next few decades. I mean not that the landscape may vanish, but that it may be diminished to something far less than it is and ought to be.

First, the Park contains 30,000 people who try to make a living from its land. The soil is thin, poor, acid, and high; business is very bad at the quarries; the economy is chronically depressed; the communities are bled by depopulation, by the country-to-town drift that divorces men from their environment and their heritage. Superimposed on the usual Park-administration problem of protecting the land and the life of the land, therefore, is the overriding problem of protecting the residents and preserving their rural culture, without which the Park would lose its essential Welsh character.

Second, the Park is only a few hours' drive from a huge cluster of cities—the sort of place where nearly seven-eighths of Britain's people live. The number of cars in Britain has more than doubled in the past ten years. Easily accessible British countryside is thus certain to be overrun by city-fleeing hordes, and indeed invaded by semipermanent centres and bases that bring still more of the city into the country and encourage the already rapid growth of active outdoor pursuits. If, furthermore, the fabric of the land is wild and fragile, and the terrain so compressed that the visitors are funneled into a few small areas, the pressure of tourism becomes a grimly literal force: the delicate earth is simply worn away by the trampling of millions of feet.

Third, steep and rainy mountains are ideal places for reservoirs and hydroelectric schemes; many of the Park's 250-odd lakes have already been tampered with or are actually artificial. Sparsely populated wildlands are also convenient places to put unpopular projects such as nuclear power stations, which, we are told, are perfectly safe but somehow not safe enough to put near large cities. Since there are already too many people in a small island nation, and since we seem to think we can go on doubling everything without limit, we shall need more and more water and electricity. Many such developments must then come—into the Park—as the logical consequence of our folly, and we can only try to choose the sites least evil for the landscape; yet each encroachment, however peripheral and controlled, impoverishes us further.

Fourth, mining consortia are starting to realize that Snowdonia is probably the most heavily mineralized area in Britain.

The combination of a potential bonanza for the shareholders and magnates, possible foreign-exchange savings for a hard-pressed Exchequer, and promised jobs for the unemployed residents can be an almost unassailable political juggernaut. The mining company now most actively prospecting in the Park has already convinced many of its residents that a rape by any other name would be a blessing.

Fifth, the fragmentation of the Park's administrative structure makes it nearly impossible to meet these threats with effective and concerted planning. The fault here is not in the men who run the Park but in the law they administer, and in the assumptions on which that law is based.

It would be both naïve and deceptive to pretend that the problems of the Park are simple, or all of the same urgency, or all on the same time-scale. The critical issues flow freely both across the Park boundaries and across the years, which pass swiftly while the Park and the Park idea are increasingly imperiled. And the interlocking of economic and scenic factors is very intricate in a landscape of which, superficially at least, man and his flocks are the main architects.

But although the answers are complex, the questions are less so, and they must be asked now if the Park is to live on as an island of wildness. Only the people of Britain can save Snowdonia: and only if they want to, only if they will bear the cost. All good things cost money. A small country cannot have a large National Park simply by defining one: she must pay for it, and pay heavily, for if it is worth having a Park it is worth having a good one. Our grandchildren, at any rate, would agree.

I think Snowdonia is an important place and its wildness an important idea. The importance in both cases extends far beyond Britain. I want therefore to tell how the land has come to be the way it is, what is happening and may happen to it, and what can be done for it. It is in a sense a microcosm of all National Parks, and of all wild places, everywhere, trying to survive too many people and too little love.

PHILIP EVANS: *Gull, Cwm Idwal*

Ond gofyn yn awr i'r anifeiliaid, a hwy a'th ddysgant;
ac i ehediaid yr awyr, a hwy a fynegant i ti.
Neu dywed wrth y ddaear, a hi a'th ddysg; a physgod y
môr a hysbysant i ti.
But ask now the beasts, and they shall teach thee;
and the fowls of the air, and they shall tell thee:
Or speak to the earth, and it shall teach thee:
and the fishes of the sea shall declare unto thee.
—JOB 12:7-8

Full many a glorious morning have I seen
Flatter the mountain tops with sovereign eye,
Kissing with golden face the meadows green,
Gilding pale streams with heavenly alchemy. . . .

—SHAKESPEARE

Blodau'r Grug

Tlws eu tw', liaws tawel,—gemau teg
   Gwmwd haul ac awel,
Crog glychau'r creigle uchel,
   Fflur y main, ffiolau'r mêl.

—Eifion Wyn (1867-1926)

Heather

They grow so comely, a quiet host, fine gems
   Of the shire of sun and breeze,
   Bells hanging from high rock places,
   Flowers of the stone, phials of honey.

—*translated by* Anthony Conran

Unless we think of intangible values as no less important than material resources, unless we are willing to say that man's need of and right to what the parks and wildernesses provide are as fundamental as any of his material needs, they are lost. . . .

—JOSEPH WOOD KRUTCH

2. Residents

WHATEVER WAYS may be devised to protect Snowdonia, the basis of the solution must ultimately be economic. I must make that clear at the start. Fresh air, as the people will tell you with sadness, is very nice, but it doesn't feed the children.

Depopulation—the steady aching drain to the cities and to England—has been going on for a long time. The young people of the Park are often very able: Merioneth (southern of the two main counties of the Park) is said to have the highest proportion of school-leavers continuing to higher education of any British county. But those who see no future for themselves in North Wales continue to go elsewhere. About half the natives of Merioneth leave the county before they are 30, yielding a population density in Meirion only one-sixth that of Wales. The permanent population of the Park consists every year of fewer and older people, more women, and more pensioners.

Yet those who stay behind do so less from necessity than from choice. They stay because they do not want to live in Birmingham. They see the advantages of Birmingham, but they are Welsh, and predominantly Welsh-speaking in a time and place in which the use of their language seems to be increasing. They have been rooted in the soil of Gwynedd for far too many centuries to leave. If in each village there were diversified jobs, a future for the children, then there would be room for such a pride in the landscape that mining and similar invasions of the Park would have no chance. In other words, an economic solution would mean a cultural and conservationist solution. People who knew the Old Language was safe, who knew their families could build secure lives in their homeland, would have time to be stewards of the fresh air.

I have taken here the view that if a certain number of people want to continue to live on a tract of land that has ceased to support them, you must devise ways to make it support them. You can instead argue that the population must be allowed to drop to the level that the land will support with the sorts of work now available. But the second course of action would in Snowdonia be disastrous, for, as we shall see, the causes of the region's poverty would still operate if there were fewer people. In the end you would be left with tiny isolated hamlets very hard to provide with the utilities and services of the State, and their culture, the life of the whole area, would wither, while the landscape itself, the clean expanse of moorland that visitors so admire, would become an impenetrable tangle of brush and forest. All this is, to be sure, a possible course of action, or rather of inaction (and I shall have more to say about it), but I do not think it wise, practical, or necessary. I think the land can, with good planning, support its present population without itself coming to harm. To see how this might be done, we must start by looking at the ways in which the people of the Park now make a living.

Dense forest—hazel, alder, birch, ash, beech, and oak—once covered the Park up to an altitude of about 1500 feet. But when men cleared the bottomlands for agriculture, about a thousand years ago, forest-clearance began to creep up the slopes, with firmly entrenched pastoralism close behind. By the seventeenth century, the trees were gone—burned, or built into Tudor ships—and what John Muir called the "hoofed locusts" ruled over the barren and beautiful rough-grasslands that are about three-fifths of the Park today. In short, the grassy mountains of Snowdonia, however natural they may look, are in fact the result of man's drastic alterations in historical times. Although it is hard to imagine what the Park would be like in its naturally afforested state, it is also too early to tell whether the grasslands, as they are now grazed, will be ecologically stable in the long run. All we know is that they are slow-healing, prone to erosion under the deluge of some of Britain's heaviest rainfall, and too poor to support anything more than a few hardy sheep. It is the wool and meat of these sheep, raised on about 1500 hill-farms, that is probably the most important single source of income in the Park.

Lowland farms, mostly outside the Park, obviously have a great commercial advantage over the hill-farms: they have softer terrain, easier communications, a far milder climate, a richer flush of grass, and a readier source of winter-feed crops.

They can use all the modern techniques and machines that the less gentle hill-farms cannot. The hill-farms can compete successfully, therefore, only if there is some endeavour that they may carry on with unique advantage. But there are painfully few such possibilities. The hill-farms used to keep wether-sheep on the mountain all year round, but public taste since World War II has preferred small cuts of lamb to big cuts of wether-mutton—or at least so the marketing experts tell us—so the wether market is nearly extinct, the victim of manipulated fashion, and only the older breeding ewes now winter on the mountain. Highland-bred rams are very hardy, it is true, but also rather small. Highland wool is unusually tough and weatherproof, but synthetic fabrics have taken much of the wool market. There is little else to do; a hill-farm cannot live on heather-honey alone.

Economic statistics confirm what the hill-farmer already knows: that not only does he earn far less than non-farmers do, but his farm is so uneconomic to run that if it is small, it probably gives less net income than the value of his work—that is, he would be better off if he kept no stock and worked as an agricultural labourer. Even the farms whose profit has held steady in recent years have lost in real purchasing power.

The sheep-farms now depend on a government subsidy. It is not clear how this subsidy can be continued after Britain joins the Common Market. But subsidy or no, the future of hill-farming, always a marginal activity, looks bleak. The Government has not seen fit to apply to hill-farming in the Park the expertise and capital it has applied to forestry, although forestry is far less vital to the local economy.

So bad is the outlook that the long-continued tenancies of many hill-farms will soon fall in. It is common to find a 50-year-old farmer with four sons, none of whom is willing to take over the tenancy, and with five older neighbours in the same fix. This lack of assured continuity has never happened before. If an adjacent tenancy lapses, few farmers will have the capital to take it over, and so the inefficient dispersion of the small holdings will be perpetuated. The most likely buyer of the vacated land will be the Forestry Commission (about which more below) or one of its commercial competitors—groups unlikely to continue to raise sheep. And more and more fields will be simply abandoned to become water-logged, weed-ridden, and derelict. Thus the pattern of de-population and stock-reduction will slowly continue. If it is not checked we shall see first the highest farms and then the lower ones gradually emptying into the towns. It is hard to imagine what this might eventually mean, for so much are the broad moorlands a sheepscape that the end of sheep-farming would be the end of the landscape as we know it. Sheep would have to be re-introduced if the mountains were to remain visible and accessible.

Consolidation of small scattered holdings often increases efficiency, and this is the present and future pattern as the farms adapt to try to survive. In economic terms, the most promising trend is the amalgamation of highland with low-land farms, so that their complementarity of specialties may be used to best advantage. More and more of the Park will come to be farmed from lowland holdings outside it. But amalgamation, like mechanization, means a better living, or at any rate a living, for fewer people. It is not a permanent answer. The farm labour-force will continue to decline, as it has done by half in the past fifteen years, and the countryside will continue to empty.

The idea, now in its infancy, that offers the greatest long-term hope of maintaining the hill-farms is a partial shift from stock-keeping to tourist-keeping. At least half of the hill-farms are now starting to augment their income by taking in lodgers, renting tent- and caravan-sites (a caravan is what in America would be called a trailer), or selling produce or fishing-rights. Few farmers seem to feel that to profit from tourism is to admit failure in honest farming; most regard tourism as a great untapped resource. And so it is. Properly done (and we shall deal more with this later) I think it could rejuvenate the farm economy. But three obstacles stand in the farmers' way.

First, the liberal tradition of the hills makes it hard to be mercenary. Passage above the mountain wall has always been free by custom and courtesy, access through the ffridd free to those who do no harm. I know a farmer with a famous crag in his front-yard, so heavily patronized by climbers that if he charged tenpence admission he could retire in style. But he would not dream of charging for access, for he comes of a hospitable race of mountain shepherds whose tribal law was that all strangers were welcome guests in the house as long as they left their spears outside. He would never think of himself as the rural analogue of the greens-keeper on a golf-course.

Second, as a result of the generous custom of free access, the farmers do not band together to fix a standard rate for more stationary sorts of land-use such as tenting. Rates vary but are always lower than could be fairly charged and gladly paid in such fine surroundings: you usually pay fivepence or tenpence a person a night for tenting, the same for parking a car overnight, and about £0.25 a night for parking a caravan.

Finally, the appearance of the Park is protected by planning regulations that require permission for keeping more than three caravans on a farm, or for keeping caravans or tents for longer than a total of four weeks in the year. The motives and principles of the regulations are sound, but their application often seems harsh, and the rules may be tightened even further, since not all the farms that now take tents under the four-week rule can accommodate them in a way safe to public health. Many farmers want and cannot get permission to keep sites beyond the four-week limit, and wonder why the time cannot be extended to cover the peak of the summer camping season, when space is so short that people camp in swamps or sleep in their cars by the roadside. Some farmers, undeterred by the lack of advice on the legal and fiscal practicalities of setting up tourist enterprises, also want permanent tent or caravan installations, which, given a few years' preparation, could be concealed behind screens of trees.

The trees may come anyway, sooner than expected, for the Forestry Commission, a government agency unconnected with the Park, is busily buying land all over the Park by the simple method of bidding well for it when it comes on the market. The Commission wishes it could buy still more. It has a gentlemen's agreement with the Park authorities about which land could be afforested, which must not be, and which might be but only under consultation; but once afforestation is approved and started, the Commission is sole judge of what to plant, where, when, and for how long. The proceedings of the consultative panel that classifies land are not published, and are therefore the subject of much speculation. The classification agreement leaves afforestation free to proceed eventually, if it can, in about 80 per cent of the Park, and it has already covered over 11 per cent, or about 60,000 acres. Admittedly, much of that 80 per cent is above the limit (about 1600 feet) of profitable forestry, and the Commission tries to show a profit.

So far the Commission has planted about 97 per cent conifers, more than half of them spruces, for conifers grow more quickly and easily than deciduous trees and have a market about nine times as great. Given the Commission's task—to try to reduce Britain's timber imports, now costing about £400 million a year, by reversing the devastating history of deforestation—the planting of conifers is sound business. In fact, Sitka spruce, which makes up nearly half the plantings, is said to grow better in much of Gwynedd than it does on its home ground in North America. And forestry in the Park, where the Commission manages 50,000 acres as forest and owns 20,000 more, offers stable jobs, though mechanization and the use of outside contractors for work in the forests have left fewer local jobs than had been hoped.

The Forestry Commission has encountered much opposition. In its early days it made some enemies during land-acquisition (though the Commission's buying policies now make it highly respected) and was often insensitive to the visual impact of its plantings. Coniferous forests, especially of spruce, are dark-coloured and monotonous, and the former practice of planting them in stiff rectangular blocks made ugly blotches on the rolling hills. The Commission now landscapes its plantations much more carefully, despite the higher cost, rounding off corners and planting in smaller clumps that blend well into the contours. But the old block-plantings are still with us, and will be much in the public view until the felling and thinning begun recently (somewhat earlier than originally planned) have given broad scope for replanting the older forests. Meanwhile, the private commercial foresters who work on a much smaller scale in the Park (under the same zoning restrictions as the Commission) try to give their clients the best possible return on investment and are less susceptible than the Commission to public pressure, so they are doing little significant landscaping.

The often-discussed planting of the relatively uneconomic hardwoods has recently started to enrich the Commission's tracts, but should be far more extensive. Softwoods outnumber hardwoods in the Park by more than eight to one, most of those hardwoods having been there before the Commission came along, and over three-fourths of the few hardwoods now being planted are rather dully uniform stands of beeches and oaks. Economic arguments deter the Commission from planting hardwoods much more widely than as borders to hide the larger coniferous plantings, especially from roads; fortunately, similar arguments will probably keep the existing hardwoods from being converted to softwoods. But all users of the Park would like to see more hardwoods, and this will cost money that must reduce the Commission's profits and working capital. A possible ingredient of a compromise between cost and beauty is the southern beech, a hardwood which, in small experimental plantings, has recently shown economic promise. It is also fairly likely that the demand for pulp products, particularly for paper, will start to decline in twenty years as more cellulose is recycled; in that case the Commission could profitably turn more of its attention to high-quality long-rotation timber growth and to forestry for recreation and conservation.

The forests' great potential for recreation has so far been much neglected. Although government subsidies are now available for recreational amenities in forests, recreation is still widely viewed as an unprofitable overhead to commercial forestry rather than as an important part of modern forest management. The Commission does provide trails, viewpoints, and picnic facilities in many of its plantings, some of which are even set up as Forest Parks, but these facilities are surprisingly little-known and little-publicized. Few people use the fine network of forest roads and paths, or know that they are entitled to. If more forests were planted in clumps and groves, their attractiveness to people (who like to stay where one sort of scenery meets another, not in the middle of a big dark wood) would increase, and with it their already great carrying capacity. If more visitors who want to get out of the city and do not much care where they go could then be diverted into the forests, the erosion of the much more fragile mountain grasslands could be substantially reduced.

If even higher standards of landscaping are maintained, hardwood plantings expanded, and vulnerable monocultures reduced, it is hard to be critical of the presence of the Forestry Commission in the Park. Countryside is, after all, a place where things will grow. Forests, unlike mines, are a living landscape. Good forests can add greatly to the scenic and biological diversity of an already varied Park, and support an interesting system of wildlife quite different from that of the grasslands or the coastal habitats.

The Moor

It was like a church to me.
I entered it on soft feet,
Breath held like a cap in the hand.
It was quiet.
What God was there made himself felt,
Not listened to, in clean colours
That brought a moistening of the eye,
In movement of the wind over grass.

There were no prayers said. But stillness
of the heart's passions—that was praise
Enough; and the mind's cession
Of its kingdom. I walked on,
Simple and poor, while the air crumbled
And broke on me generously as bread.

—R. S. THOMAS

And as I was green and carefree, famous among the barns
About the happy yard and singing as the farm was home,
In the sun that is young once only,
Time let me play and be
Golden in the mercy of his means,
And green and golden I was huntsman and herdsman, the calves
Sang to my horn, the foxes on the hills barked clear and cold,

Another powerful sculptor of the Park's scenery, but in a less fortunate way, has been the extraction of rock from the ground, both the mining of ores and the quarrying of slates and granite. Mining—for gold, copper, lead, zinc, manganese, and even iron—has a long history in the Park, and has generally taken the form of following isolated rich veins or lodes until they petered out, which seemed to happen often. The resulting spoil-tips, often too toxic to revegetate, are to be found scattered through some of the larger new forests and in open country; occasionally the scars are more extensive, as where escaping cyanide killed plants in Nant Conwy. Since about the end of World War I, there has been no serious mining in the Park; yet we shall see later that new mining proposals, this time for diffuse low-grade ores but on a huge scale, are the most critical threat to the Park today.

Slate-quarrying has had a more obvious impact on the land and people than mining has, partly because the quarrying of the Caernarvonshire slate (the most important vein of slate in Britain, and said to be the best in the world) has been so extensive and partly because each ton of slate brings with it about seven tons of waste rock that must be put somewhere. Thus a big quarry can produce tens of tons of waste each week. From the late 1700s until World War II, quarrying was a major industry in North Wales, and brought relative prosperity to many towns, which in return became dangerously dependent on the continuing success of the quarries. But in the past twenty years, steadily dropping business and increasing mechanization have reduced the number of quarry jobs by at least a third. Only a handful of the giant quarries have been able to remain open. Some of the men have gone to work at the comparatively new and slowly expanding granite quarries, but far more are unemployed and likely to remain so, often because of industrial diseases or disabilities. The heavy welfare burden of the quarrying towns is one legacy of the failure of the slate industry; but a thousand acres of desolation make the most obvious monument to the plunder of the Park's landscape. It is remarkable that so much conspicuously derelict land should be within the Park, because the Park's boundaries were carefully drawn to exclude as much of the devastation as possible, even to the extent of omitting an entire district that would otherwise have been right in the middle. (You will see later the relevance of this point: that the sites of past mineral extraction were thought unsuited for inclusion in a National Park whose boundaries were nonetheless drawn to include large ore-bodies known to be potentially valuable.)

Though the Caernarvonshire authorities estimate that well over a square mile of quarrying dereliction in their part of the Park (the northern part) could be reclaimed, at least partly, there is no money for the work. (The County Council may, however, spend a third of a million dollars on reclamation at the edge of the Park, in connection with the Llyn Padarn project described below.) The scale of the task is immense: at several places bordering the Park, whole mountainsides have been gnawed away during two centuries and heaped up as waste. The heaps are far too big to shovel back into the pits without astronomical expense. Not even under ideal experimental conditions have the problems of revegetating the waste been fully solved; the rock is broiling hot in summer (because of its dark colour), mechanically unstable, poor in nutrients, unable to retain water, and nearly impossible to shape and spread. The best we can hope for now is to hide the ugliest of the heaps behind a pitying screen of trees—and ensure that this tearing out of the insides of the earth will not come again to the Park.

We have seen the importance and frailty of farming and quarrying as mainsprings of the Park's economy. What, then, of other jobs? It is hard to find out the rôle of town-based jobs, for the statistics are compiled only for much larger areas that include principal towns outside the Park. It is not clear how many Park residents commute by car into the towns to work, although the number is plainly rising as rural opportunities decline, and with them, in a vicious circle, rural shops and public transport.

In the entire counties of Caernarvonshire and Merioneth (only a tiny piece of the Park, mainly agricultural, is in Denbighshire), the various service, distribution, and construction industries account altogether for more than half of the total employment, and light manufacturing for another quarter, but the proportion of Park residents involved would be very much smaller—how much, nobody knows. It is known, however, that tourism is an increasingly important source of jobs in the Park, both directly and by adding enough money to the local economy to support rural shops and services that would otherwise be forced to close. The importance of tourism to the villages recently became clear when a five-month outbreak of foot-and-mouth disease restricted mountain travel and nearly shut off the flow of winter visitors; Capel Curig, the eastern gateway to Eryri, was hit by a severe recession in consequence.

The maritime climate makes it impossible to build a winter-resort pattern, although a good effort is being made to develop a winter conference-centre at Bala, and film-making units (which work best outside the regular tourist season) are starting to realize that in Meirion they can find almost any conceivable kind of terrain within a very small area. But these developments are a drop in the ocean: winter in Gwynedd is a lean season. The tourist traffic is seasonal, and so is the persistently high unemployment rate of Snowdonia, fluctuating typically from 5-8 per cent in winter to 3 per cent (in farming districts) or 5 per cent (in quarry towns) in summer. The winter figure compares unfavourably with about 4 per cent for all Wales and 2½ per cent for all Britain. And added to the strain placed on the Park area's welfare services by unemployment is that resulting from the increasing average age of residents. This is caused by both emigration of the young and immigration of the old, often from England, who want to retire in little rural cottages. Thus while the population of the Park shrinks, the number of pensioners in the Park grows. This shift of constitution can only reinforce the present pattern of decline.

The industrial future of the Park does not lie in heavy industry. What heavy industry is spreading from England and South Wales seems to be going to the north coast and to Anglesey, which has better sea, rail, and road links than do the mainland counties. Recent Governments have offered various inducements to heavy industries willing to move to North Wales. (For example, I understand that the new Rio Tinto alumina-smelting plant on Anglesey, which will use an amount equal to roughly half the output of Anglesey's new nuclear power station, will get its electricity at what is effectively a special rate subsidized by the State. The plant was also built on specially cheap land and at a subsidized cost.) But I fear that those conventional light industries that are following the larger factories to the mainland—mostly on the north coast— are in the long run not the right answer either. They are usually run by and for Englishmen; they are highly disruptive to the environment, or the village-based culture, or both; and they are vulnerable, the first to close in a recession, just when they are most needed.

The Park's Planning Consultant, Professor J. S. Allen, recently said: "I am strongly supporting any move for industry to be introduced into the National Park which is suitable for a National Park. . . . I would like to see the kind of employment in which the young child at school can study at school with the hope of getting progressive employment, with progressive promotion, within his own county. That is very different from providing a few years' work for the lower-paid workers of the county who will then at the end of the period of employment go back on the dole. I am looking for permanent employment. . . ." What the Park area needs, then, is small, easily assimilated, locally based businesses offering a broad enough spectrum of opportunities to persuade young people to stay—and preferably making some use of the Park's huge reservoir of intelligent uncommitted women, most of whom would work if they had the chance. There are many steadily expanding industries so light as to be almost cottage industries, but calling on more or less sophisticated skills: for example, specialized engraving and printing, scientific instrumentmaking, light machining and engineering, editing and proofreading, electronic assembly and repair, computer programming, and a whole new class of "paperwork industries"—administrative and bookkeeping divisions decentralized from their parent companies, and doing work that, while it depends on sound postal and telephonic links, does not have to be in the same county as the day-to-day plant operations. There is no reason why a large company on the north coast could not put many of its desk-workers in a more attractive village farther inland.

Little effort is now being made to attract, or better yet to start locally, small non-disruptive industries of these sorts. (Professor Allen has mentioned one notable exception, a small factory that makes high-quality brass wood-screws.) But in default of hill-farming, diversified cottage-industry-like endeavours are the only way to hold the patterns of rural life together while compensating for the seasonal efforts of tourism.

3. Visitors

TOURISM brought more than £80 million ($200 million) to Wales in 1967—a higher per-capita figure than in any country in the world except Switzerland and Austria, and 5.5 times the per-capita figure for the whole United Kingdom. A sixth of this Welsh income went to the Snowdonia National Park. Tourism is expanding, indeed exploding, in the Park: especially in the past two or three years, tourism has grown so suddenly that it is hard to estimate how many visitors there are. It is suggestive that about half a million people each year try to ascend Yr Wyddfa, which is only one of the Park's many attractions; that over 400,000 annually visit the Swallow Falls, a pleasant but not extraordinary cascade by the side of the main east road into the Park; and that during the summer peak, at least 400,000 visitors stay in Wales each night, a number equal to 15 per cent of the Welsh population.

Yet the Park authorities, finding themselves the curators of an increasingly valuable and sought-after commodity, are caught between two temptations. If they encourage tourism in such a way that more people who do not respect the land are likely to visit it, the Park will be ruined. Even now, tourists' erosion, litter, and trespass are very serious problems. To let tourism continue to expand in as uncontrolled a fashion as at present—an almost inescapable course under the Park's current administrative structure—would be to invite disaster. If, on the other hand, tourism is discouraged or regulated too harshly, if the laudable impulse to preserve the landscape becomes too inflexibly hostile to accept the idea of tourism as a constructive force, then the Park will also die, perhaps more slowly but just as surely, from the strangle of poverty that we have already discussed.

I think tourism can be guided in such a way that it does not destroy the land or the people; I am sure it is possible to instil a wider sympathy for the life and needs of the countryside into those who come to it; I regard planned tourism under sound management as the greatest potential resource of the Park, and the only resource that does not fade or weaken or run out. But making the Park's beauty produce the Park's bread will not be easy or inexpensive. Ensuring that tourism does not destroy the Park as it tries to become self-supporting will require a national popular commitment to the National Park idea: that is, a national conviction that Parks are both a need and a responsibility.

It will also require a change of attitude among the people of the Park, for they have a saying, "We can't live on scenery." They can live on scenery, just as the natives of other beautiful places do, if only they realize it is possible—and if they let the scenery live—but first they must see what sort of scenery they have. It is notoriously hard to perceive beauty close to home, and in any event the greatest creative sensitivity and imagination of the Welsh have traditionally been in other spheres than the visual; the visual scene is seldom regarded as a medium to be responsibly altered in accordance with artistic wishes. Nor have more than a handful of those few residents who know their own land well travelled widely in other lands. Fundamental to a sense of husbandry is a sense of identity and significance. Until the people of the Park see that their land is more than just a pretty place, that its beauty indeed is important to the whole world, I do not see how they can be willing or able to make their stewardship profitable, or how they can be expected to defend scenery that they do not yet view as their best long-range source of livelihood.

It is an unpalatable truth that there is little local commercial initiative in the Park. For example, city tourists naturally want well-made country crafts; there are in the Park some exceedingly gifted craftsmen, especially in slate and stone; yet almost all of the existing crafts-shops (so-called) sell little more than trinkets and curios—and are run by Englishmen. And the Park authorities, who see what could be done with the talent available, are not legally empowered to take any effective action to encourage local cottage industry.

To speak bluntly, in the twenty years in which it has been clear that the Park could save itself from a dreadful fate (which could have come in various forms but turns out to be mining) only by developing a strong tourist industry, there has been almost no concerted effort to do so. Natural reticence and a vacillation between philosophies of development and of preservation have combined to retard growth, and the few efforts made have been sporadic, uncoördinated, unprofessional, and only moderately successful. Now that the relevant officials know what sorts of income might be had and what developments are most needed, both the machinery for sowing a native tourist industry and the leisure for bringing it to maturity are lacking. The power to sow, indeed, has never existed, even though it is obvious to everyone that enterprises will not arise spontaneously but must be encouraged and nurtured. Recent legislation that could in theory be used for this purpose has not been so used. The eager volunteers who are rejuvenating some of the narrow-gauge railways of Gwynedd would in any sensible régime be aided by the Government's development agencies, for the railways are showing a steady 10 per cent annual growth rate and now make over 800,000 passenger-journeys a year; yet this splendid chance for public or private investment is languishing while the amateurs struggle on as best they can.

. . . it seems to me particularly good that there is still a calling
in which everything depends on the weather, the sky, the cold, the clouds,
so many "things" which have nothing to do with automation.
Automation is rational and undoubtedly clever
but it is in danger of withering us up unless we find good compensations.

The results of this universal neglect of opportunity are easy to see. Visitors to the Park still spend relatively little money there; this is especially regrettable because tourists' money circulates rapidly and has a strong snowballing effect on the local economy. Because it is often inconvenient to buy food in the Park, most tenting and caravanning tourists bring their food with them, spending locally only a third as much money as hotel- and motel-occupants do. Visitors cannot buy first-rate local crafts as they would like to do; they cannot easily find out much more of the local history than the story of Gelert's grave; on rainy days and in the evenings there is no-where for them to go (there are hardly any local museums); at night and on Sundays they have trouble finding a place to eat; they cannot get the excellent local food, but only standard English commercial cooking; there is almost no system of grading or reservations for guest-houses and hotels; the diffi-culty of crossing barriers of culture and language to meet any Welshmen induces a feeling of depressed isolation, a feeling intensified by the bleakly deserted mood of the towns at night. Even when visitors are exploring the Park, they have little idea how to get the most benefit from their visit, and have practically no wardens or local information-booths to con-sult. Those tourists who climb Snowdon might as well be climbing a big block of concrete, for all the notice they take of the fossils under their feet.

Despite these inconveniences, tourists by the millions do come to the Park, most of them repeatedly. To understand the impact that they have and will have on the Park, we must ask many questions: who are they? where are they from? why and how do they come? where do they stay? what do they do?

Many years ago, the only visitors to Snowdonia were a few English gentlemen who were gladly given the freedom of the hills, for they were guests and friends. Though there are those who refuse to see it, the days of the few and of the gentlemen are long gone and will not return. These are the days of the many, the hurrying, the strangers, the unknowing and all too often uncaring townsmen. They seek and find recreation in the countryside without having to pay for it. The residents find themselves the involuntary (and sometimes reluctant) proprietors of a vast amusement-park which they own and pay for but which the visitors put to their own use, sometimes well, often badly. This is not a satisfactory state of affairs, both because it is unfair for the residents to bear the sole cost and because the countryside is being damaged. It is too facile to say that education will remedy abuses. Education does not pick up litter (a little learning, however, may too often en-courage us to collect specimens of the rare plants that it teaches us to recognize). Of course we need education, and it must be better done than it is now; but if we complacently suppose that it will solve the problems of rural recreation then we have missed the point—the Park's urgent need for manage-ment meanwhile.

The main villain of the Park's recent history is the private automobile, which brings eight or nine out of every ten visi-tors today. In the winter, the people of Capel Curig cannot sleep from about eight o'clock Friday night to one o'clock Saturday morning, for there are too many cars whizzing by their windows, taking English weekenders into Eryri. On Sunday night the flow reverses. In the summer, all thoughts of weekend inconveniences are submerged in a tidal wave of visitors. Over half of these are family groups on holiday, out for a stroll and some snapshots, but many are day-trippers (from the West Midlands and Merseyside conurbations or from Wales itself) who use the car simply as an extension of the home—they often go into the countryside to read the 'paper or eat a meal or listen to the radio or go to sleep.

Welsh topography is better suited to horses and mules than to cars. The roads, despite continuing local improvements, are and will remain narrow, steep, and winding; the best of them will never be as good as a modest road in the flatlands. Hence certain places are the sites of continuous traffic-jams that last nearly all summer. There is no traffic-management plan for the Park, nor (at present) any hope of making one. The intense traffic congestion is aggravated by the use of the roads through the mountains, especially the A5, as main trunk highways carrying through traffic—a pattern that destroys the Park's traditional position as not a means of getting to someplace else, but a serene end in itself.

Increasing industrialization of Anglesey (which the A5 links with much of England) and intensification of Anglesey's sea trade, especially with Ireland, are certain to raise the volume of heavy through-traffic. Even though the heavy-vehicle problem is already serious, the existing legal machinery for restricting traffic in the Park has not been exercised—that would need the consent of the Minister of Transport. In the early days of motoring, the A5's relatively direct route was rather quicker than the coastal route around the north side of the mountains, but faster roads now make it doubtful that the difference is significant, and the coast's better climate would in the long run be a more important criterion. Although the Government's road-development policy for Snowdonia is not yet clear, it is likely that the folly of channeling through traffic into the already-clogged inland valleys will be continued and reinforced. There is also a proposal for building an elaborate direct link from the Rhyl-Prestatyn area to the northeastward, thus bringing the mountains even closer to the cities and making it much easier to come to the Park for a day or part of a day. It would seem to many people that a more sensible course would be to sort out the present acute problems of overcrowding in the Park before multiplying them. I do not look forward to the day when even faster roads will link the Park to a giant city stretching from Liverpool to London.

It is the car, and to a lesser extent the ever-more-easily-afforded minibus and hired coach, that have brought the once-isolated Park within reach of the nation, for the public transport is quite inadequate (mainly because it cannot compete with cars). A recent survey showed that just over half of the summer visitors had driven more than 120 miles—about three hours—to come to the Park, and nearly a third had come from at least the distance of London, roughly five or six hours away. It is to lessen this tedious commuting that many groups of visitors have established semipermanent bases in or just outside the Park, generally by converting disused cottages or farm-buildings: there are now half-a-dozen Youth Hostels, close to two dozen main huts owned by mountaineering clubs, and nearly thirty full-time residential centres for outdoor pursuits and field studies. These outdoor centres are usually owned by county or city educational authorities, and are used for a spectrum of activities ranging from adventurous mountain training to academic field ecology. Eryri is said to have the highest concentration of outdoor study centres of any area in the world.

The use of these bases during the academic year has brought heavier foot-traffic in the mountains. This has greatly increased erosion, especially in the classic teaching areas and on the most popular high paths, because the mountains no longer have a chance to heal themselves during the winter and early spring. Every day now, even in bad weather, large organized parties go over the paths, giving them no respite. And although skiing is not likely to become a major activity in the Park, winter climbing during the December-to-April season will continue to grow: fewer than half of the Park's obvious snow-and-ice routes have had their first ascents.

The Small Window

In Wales there are jewels
To gather, but with the eye
Only. A hill lights up
Suddenly; a field trembles
With colour and goes out
In its turn; in one day
You can witness the extent
Of the spectrum and grow rich

With looking. Have a care;
This wealth is for the few
And chosen. Those who crowd
A small window dirty it
With their breathing, though sublime
And inexhaustible the view.

—R. S. THOMAS

PHILIP EVANS: *Tryfan, Llyn Ogwen*

*It is the extension of transport without a corresponding growth of perception
that threatens us with qualitative bankruptcy of the recreational process.
Recreational development is a job not of building roads into lovely country,
but of building receptivity into the still unlovely human mind.*
—ALDO LEOPOLD

Active mountain pursuits (as opposed to mere sightseeing) have been carried on in one way by both resident and visiting mountaineers for many decades, but are now the province also of a rapidly expanding class of students and instructors with widely varying interests. Many of these mountain-users are based in the area full-time but few are natives, and surprisingly few are even countrymen or mountaineers. Some are simply physical-education teachers taking advantage of a free outdoor playground. The mountains are the losers. Even the professional mountaineering instructors, who are almost the only force for maintaining the finest traditions of their way of life, find it hard to reconcile conservation practice with theory. At a highly respected centre in the Park, for example, you may hear an instructor give an excellent lecture on keeping the hills clean; but the same man, when his party has struck camp in Cwm Bochlwyd, is not likely to refill the drainage trenches, or

The space available in the national parks is not big enough for all who want to use them.
But the size of a park is directly related to the manner in which you use it.
If you are in a canoe traveling at three miles an hour, the lake on which you are paddling
is ten times as long and ten times as broad as it is to the man in a speedboat going thirty.
. . . Every road that replaces a footpath, every outboard motor
that replaces a canoe paddle, shrinks the area of the park.

—Paul Brooks

replace the boulders with which the flysheets and tent-pegs have been weighted, and it will not occur to him that he has disturbed the landscape in a far more obvious and permanent way than by simple littering. It is only in the past two years, when high camping by organized groups has increased so markedly, that the first traces of detergent-suds have started to appear in the streams.

Tenting is the most popular form of overnight accommodation in the Park, with caravans a distant second. Large sites for both—for example, in Forest Parks and coastal commercial developments respectively—are heavily used, indeed are packed full in the summers, but do not satisfy the desire of many visitors to camp deep in the country. Authorized space on farms is very limited. The result is that many caravans stay overnight or even for days on end by the roadside, in spaces intended for short stops by drivers; and tents are erected on valley sites in ways injurious to the land or dangerous to public health. (The notorious tenting situation in the toilet-less Llanberis Pass is a public scandal.) Sound primitive tent-sites are clearly a need of high priority, and would permit the most hazardous unofficial sites to be closed, but for reasons we shall see later, very little has so far been done. Nor does there seem to be any Park-wide planning on where to put the rising number of tents and caravans so that they will do the least damage to the land and its beauty. Many people think the Park is already saturated by caravans, for which there are 20,000 spaces in or near the Park, some attractive and some not. Yet on a matter on which a policy is so essential, none has been made. There is no clear standard of how well-hidden, well-managed, or peripheral a site must be in order to be acceptable. There does seem to be a bias in favour of tents; it would be more of a hardship to tenters than to caravanners to be sited outside the Park, since the latter always have cars.

To a surprising extent the mountains can be protected by diversionary tactics—by giving people more things to do near the roads but not improving access to land farther away. Many visitors, especially in the summer, do not want to go high up, but want only to park somewhere and enjoy the view from the road, or perhaps take a short low-level stroll. The local authorities concerned are well aware that there ought to be more parking- and stopping-places, picnic facilities, litter-bins, toilets, and other amenities for the ubiquitous car-borne visitor. (Improvements of this sort, such as the Milestone Buttress parking-area, seem well done.) It is therefore gratifying that such improvements may, if various committees approve and if the Treasury is feeling prosperous, obtain a 75 per cent State subsidy. But there are two ways of looking at this grant: first, that the local councils are getting at a quarter of the usual cost a chance to build improvements that will increase the county's tourist revenue; second, that the visitors, most of whom are from well outside the Park, are paying nothing for the public services they receive, while the local ratepayers, whose rates are often very high indeed, are paying a quarter of the bill. Residents of the Park are likely to take the latter view, and to be ambivalent toward projects that are clearly necessary but that are also impositions from without.

It is the residents who pay for not only the presence but also the thoughtlessness of visitors. The damage done is diverse, but most of it falls under three headings—litter, trespass, and erosion—and all of it except erosion is ascribable to an urban-rural lack of communication.

Litter is a permanent problem of all countryside peripheral to cities, but it is especially harmful in the Park because the bare ground makes it so obvious and because many commonly discarded objects, such as tins, can seriously injure livestock. The litter-bins along the roads are too few, too small, and too seldom emptied to keep up with the filling, particularly in the summer, when campers and hut-occupants (and local ratepayers with campers on their land) add to the usual load. Here again, local councils are being asked to pay for cleaning up after visitors who will not pay their own way. To make matters worse, the bins are so designed that wind, crows, and gulls can remove any rubbish that has not already overflowed, whereupon the wind redistributes it back over the landscape. The resulting messiness is not conducive to high public standards. Even when volunteer groups clean up a mountain and carry all the litter down to the road, the litter is almost as likely to blow away again as to be collected. Local entrepreneurs cannot start a bin-emptying business (for which the money could be found) because the law requires collections to be made by the local public-health authorities.

Trespass—or access, depending on your viewpoint—is rather a broad term: strictly speaking, very little of the Park is public property, and all who roam in the hills are therefore trespassing on somebody's land. But many visitors think that since the land is called a National Park it must be national property where citizens have a legal right to wander whither they will, and this error has led to a great deal of ill-feeling. Vocal and misinformed civil-liberties claimants would make it very hard to close temporarily an area that needed a chance to heal.

The actual ownership of the Park is very diffused: almost 75 per cent of the land belongs to private persons (a great many of them), 13 per cent to the Forestry Commission, an important and fairly well protected 8 per cent to the National Trust (a private government-chartered conservation group that manages its tracts in order to preserve their scenic values for the public benefit), 4 per cent to the Secretary of State for Wales (the Vaynol Estate purchase, to be discussed later), and small tracts to other corporations and agencies. (One of these is the Nature Conservancy, a government agency that conducts scientific research on the structure and function of the land; it owns or leases, and usually opens to the public, excellent examples of the various types of terrain found in the Park. It is from the Conservancy's work that ways of making the hill-farms more profitable and the paths more durable are most likely to emerge.)

Almost no farmers refuse to grant access across their land, so long as the arrangement is voluntary and terminable if abused—tolerance is largely a question of numbers. The exist-ing rules for obtaining compulsory access orders have never yet been used in the Park, and there are only a few places (e.g., the Nantlle area, the back of Y Garn from Nant Peris, the Carneddau from near Helyg) where access is not normally granted. But the farmers' patience is sorely tried by those few visitors who leave gates open, climb dry-stone walls, enter hayfields, fondle newborn lambs, bring dogs onto sheep-walks, and otherwise make thorough nuisances of themselves. These misdeeds generally result not from malice but from simple ignorance about agriculture and the countryside. This ignorance is not adequately dispelled by on-the-spot propaganda. The Country Code, a sort of Ten Commandments for countrygoers, is very good of its kind, but rubs some people the wrong way and is more known than obeyed by many more. (Modern man does not like to read, let alone obey, lists of rules: pictures are better, at least for attracting attention to public notices. Requests should be explained, not stated baldly without a reason. The abominable habits of "forbidding" things and of quoting from statutes should be forbidden; they act as a goad, nearly as irresistible as a "Wet Paint" sign.)

The rare farmer who has suffered serious loss can seldom find out who is to blame, though resident centres harbour the most easily identifiable hill-users and are the easiest to complain to. Army bases and a few other hill-users have liaison officers who keep track of which parties go where; a similar service for visiting school parties is badly needed, and is being sought by the Park authorities. But as matters stand, farmers just have to bear the losses and try to educate the public as

AMORY LOVINS: Idwal Slabs

best they can. Hill-farmers are remarkably well-disposed and forgiving people, but relations, like stone walls, are more easily broken than mended.

The loosening and breaking of the old walls is an especially sad type of rural damage, for the money and skill to rebuild the walls can rarely be found, and makeshift wire fences are the result. They are not beautiful, and grow less so with age; mice and birds cannot nest in them, nor lichens grow on them, nor sheep and people shelter behind them, nor scenery blend with them. There is no warmth or heart in wire fences, only a bit of taut twisted metal that scrapes and jangles in the wind. The loss of many of the fine walls in Llanberis Pass has greatly reduced its beauty, for even in awesome terrain, it is the bit of ugliness just in front of you that will catch your eye.

Trail erosion is becoming desperately critical in the Park, and the few groups of enthusiastic volunteers who work on the paths have recently been overwhelmed by the work needed. I can remember paths that three years ago were faint sheep-tracks, blurs that could be followed only with constant attention and a bit of divine inspiration. Now they are squelching gullies six feet wide and two deep. The mechanism is simple: once the grass is so trampled that its roots can no longer bind the soil, the path becomes muddy, so people walk by the side of it. The same process is then repeated until the path has become a stream, then—depending on the steepness—a morass or a gully, and finally either a huge swamp or the cause of a landslip. The basis of the problem is too many people, going in too few places (a result of the very steep terrain, which concentrates both the damage and the drainage), during too much of the year, on thin grass with torrential rainfall, high humidity, and extensive freeze-thaw cycles. The size of the problem is shown by the numbers: of the roughly 500,000 people who try, each year, to converge on one square yard atop Yr Wyddfa, nearly four-fifths go on foot (the rest wait, sometimes for hours, to get a seat on the cog railway); and of those 400,000-odd, about 300,000 are divided between two of the six main footpaths. Even though only about half the hikers succeed, the wear is bound to be severe. Traffic and erosion are nearly as heavy on the steep ground under several popular climbing crags, e.g., at Tremadoc, Dinas y Gromlech, and the Idwal Slabs.

There is a great irony in the poor state of the major paths in Eryri. Many of them were built and paved for mule- and pony-borne tourists just after the Napoleonic Wars, and they were splendid. Other fine paths linked the mines to their village labour-supplies. But all these paths were allowed to fall into ruin when labour became scarce and mines closed. The legacy of neglect is ours, and we are compounding it.

An urgent priority in Park management must be the building and maintenance of properly drained gravel- and rock-filled footpaths, wide enough for two to walk abreast, at the points of heaviest erosion. The cost would not be excessive, and the money and the will to use it must be found promptly

PHILIP EVANS: On Bristly Ridge

if catastrophic gullying and land-slippage are to be averted. (I think people hiking up Snowdon would gladly pay a five-penny or tenpenny toll to help make the paths passable—if the local authorities allowed such a toll to be levied, which at present they will not.) Once paths were built, forcing people to keep to them would be as unnecessary as it would be undesirable; very few people have any wish to stray from the recognized routes, which usually follow the best lines—sometimes the only lines negotiable without hip-boots or skyhooks.

Waymarking is an urgent need related to both trail erosion and trespass. Almost all of the local residents want four types of improvements which they themselves neither can nor should pay for. First, if farmers were given a small financial incentive they could mark the route, and especially the stiles, for getting up to the mountain wall through the bottomland and ffridd. At present this is almost never done, so it is no wonder that town-trained visitors often stray and do damage. Above the mountain wall, the customary major routes should also be marked where they are too indistinct to be readily followed and where the land is especially fragile. It is important to remember that while townsmen would have trouble following any unmarked moorland or mountain path, they are not the only ones: fairly skilled mountaineers unused to sheepwalks may be equally perplexed. Second, several narrow valleys and passes must have footpaths by which pedestrians can avoid the heavy motor traffic that thunders along the icy and foggy roads. Third, both safety and trail-protec-

Pre-Cambrian

I call this patch of vantage by your name:
A country of worn and as if courteous rock
That yields no secret easily, yet
In which birch grows shapely, multiplying fern
Hang round clear pools; where light is always
Dawn's timeless cantabile . . . A shallow country,
Dappled by age to be a sunning spot for lizards
And I, an intruder, casting so long a shadow
It snaps their moss landscape shut, like a fan.

—ANTHONY CONRAN

PHILIP EVANS: Detail, top of stone wall, Watkin Path

tion would be served if there were easy low-level strolling routes, marked and described by information-boards, for keeping car-based non-mountaineers and keen-but-infirm hikers happily occupied in diverse terrain, off the high routes, and out of trouble. Suiting terrain near the roads to the needs of the less active visitors is a good way to protect the wilder uplands from over-use. Finally, some of the popular high paths should be better marked where it is easy to stray onto subtly dangerous ground, e.g., on Llwybr y Mul below Bwlch Glas. This marking must be very carefully done if it is not to tempt eager tourists onto ground for which they are unprepared, as is happening with many of the freshly marked Glyder routes. It is no good having alluring and uninformative way-markings at the base of the mountain, followed by a deteriorating path that leads to unexpected difficulties or obscurities late in the day. Paint-marking of cairns on Glyder Fach could have been both clearer and less obtrusive; this form of way-marking is widely used in other areas, especially in America, and if it is to be used more widely, it would be worth calling on the skills of people accustomed to the craft.

Mountain safety is an old problem in the Park, and it is not getting any better: an increase in hiking accidents is more than balancing a decrease in climbing accidents. The eight civilian mountain-rescue teams, even though they are not properly subsidized by the State and are always short of money for much-needed equipment, are extremely efficient, and usually manage to give silly people an undeserved chance to repeat their mistakes. (Searches are often aided by the excellent helicopter-equipped RAF team from Anglesey—full compensation for the annoyance of low-level jet training flights through the Park's narrow valleys.) Despite intensive efforts at public education, one still sees a great many plainly incompetent parties doing foolish things on the hills. They all think—those who give it a thought—that it won't happen to them. They cannot all be right. In the winter of 1969-70, at least seven people died on just the Snowdon massif.

I am sorry to say that among the most frequent offenders against common sense are school parties. They are often too large, badly shod and equipped, and looked after by a master who did a bit of hill-walking twenty years ago but has no idea that leading a group of young people is a very different, and a very serious, business. The current record for a single party is said to be 198 schoolchildren accompanied by one master; the highest ratio I have seen is 112:1, on Crib Goch. No doubt there are schoolmasters who are skilled and conscientious mountain guides, but somehow one seldom seems to meet them. Nonetheless I am sorry to have to single them out, especially because, coroners' strictures about winter climbing in high-heeled shoes to the contrary, many highly experienced mountaineers have got into trouble in Eryri. Experience is not the only quality needed for safety.

I do not know the answer to this problem. If a local guide writes a mild letter to the headmaster of a school whose party he has just extricated from some stupid fix, the reply is likely to be apoplectic. Very few parents know what is at stake. I hope it does not take a calamity—many of which have already been averted by some mountaineer's providential presence—to improve the standard of leadership of organized parties. The parents deserve better. Fixing a statutory maximum size or boy-to-man ratio for organized parties, as has become necessary in parts of northern New England, may help but not fundamentally.

Requiring schoolmasters (or others) to have formal mountain-leadership credentials is not a solution. The currently available British certificate of this sort can be obtained by any competent 20-year-old on the basis of a week's assessment preceded by a week of rudimentary instruction and by a year's occasional field experience. I do not think the certificate is worthless—it is good as far as it goes—but there is a danger that people who obtain it will think, or convince others, that it means they are competent to lead parties, and that is not true. I understand that the professional guides of Snowdonia have equally little confidence in recently proposed extensions of this certificate. Some of the higher grades of instructors' accreditation now available do require a high standard of technical competence, and give some opportunity for testing the soundness of a candidate's judgment, but schoolmasters are unlikely to try to obtain such credentials, which are intended for aspirant guides.

If full-time professional wardens become active on the mountains of the Park, an excellent deterrent would be to vest in those wardens who have long experience of local guiding a statutory power to order off the mountains any organized party that is being led in a grossly negligent and highly dangerous way. It should also be made possible to arrange for the educational authorities to invoke sanctions against the school or master involved. Something must certainly be done to reduce the present waste not only of life but also of manpower: there are times now when one team of volunteers must run three rescues in a single day, all avoidable.

One of the few bright spots in the mountain scene is that little serious damage is being caused by high-level camping. To a large extent the mountains are their own guardians, for those few people willing and equipped to brave the high storms are mostly conservation-minded. As far as I know there is only one high refuge-hut in the whole Park, and no prospect of more, so high camping by the unequipped will not be encouraged. What the Park notably lacks as an amenity for mountaineers is any sort of Alpine-style hut open to all: not a hostel or a club-hut, but a public valley refuge with sitting-space and good simple food. The two best potential sites for such a public amenity have just been diverted to other, more private, uses, very worthwhile in their own spheres but benefitting only a rather small segment of the public. A comprehensive development plan for the Park, if there were one, would, I think, have made a wiser compromise.

4. Exploiters

THE SNOWDONIA NATIONAL PARK was set up to preserve and enhance the natural beauty and to promote public enjoyment of an area specially suited to such use by reason of its natural beauty and the opportunities it affords for open-air recreation, having regard both to character and to position in relation to centres of population. In this definition (paraphrased from the 103-page National Parks and Access to the Countryside Act, 1949) lie the seeds of the destruction of the Park's wildness. The short distance from cities that has made the Park such a desirable playground—a distance soon, perhaps, to be further shrunk by the Dee Barrage and other road developments—may also let public enjoyment, if uncontrolled, attain a level that will amount to public conquest and pillage. But the cities affect the Park in more ways than by merely overrunning it with visitors.

The pressures of population on the Park take many forms. In the long run, those forms of damage that are obvious, local, and direct (such as trail-erosion and wall-destruction) can be remedied, given a moderate fund of money and goodwill, and differ little in principle from the normal wear and tear felt by other National Parks throughout the world. A danger far more subtle, pervasive, and powerful comes from the disguised pressures on the Park to divert its land-uses from recreation and agriculture; pressures, in short, to become something other, and less, than a National Park.

For both economic and political reasons, the Park is peculiarly susceptible to interference with its traditional patterns of land-use. The economic depression of North Wales has bedevilled many successive Governments, none of which has met with much success. As we have seen, the Park is very short of jobs; any development that seems to promise them is therefore likely to be welcomed rather than uncritically. Furthermore, projects for exploiting the Park are likely to originate outside Wales, in England or overseas, and thus to have behind them a great deal of eco-political influence, capital, and momentum—advantages that Wales, and especially the sparsely populated farmlands of North Wales can neither enjoy nor combat. Many North Welshmen feel, with a good deal of justice, that their interests are often subordinated to those of the industrial South, and, more importantly, the interests of Wales as a whole to those of England. Welsh autonomy is increasing, but however eloquent her spokesmen may be, Wales will never have many votes in Parliament.

Private citizens who try to defend any National Park against blatantly commercial exploitation face not only special regional handicaps such as these, but also many others found everywhere. First, most development schemes are secretly worked out long in advance, and are publicized only after such massive financial and political interests have been drawn into them that effective resistance is difficult, if indeed there is time to organize any. Next, it is common for a prospective developer to confer privately ahead of time with each of the people and groups likely to oppose his plans, and to reassure each by telling him what he hopes to hear. (Interviewing some of the men involved in the present mineral exploration of the Park leaves me with a strong impression that this lubrication has already been done, very thoroughly and adroitly.) Next, the developer is usually out to make a large investment and profit, and does not begrudge a proportionately small sum—say half a million pounds—for insurance in the form of legal and public-relations expertise.

Next, the volunteer organizations that defend Parks and their flora and fauna tend, especially in Britain, to be small, underfinanced, and specialized, and hence are not effective enough and are often represented as a handful of eccentrics. Conservationists from outside the endangered area can all be labelled as selfish foreigners interested in their own benefit rather than the residents'. The Government agencies responsible for or interested in the Parks have clearly defined assignments (seldom including any assignment to make gratuitous comments on private companies' plans for self-enrichment) and usually lack strict jurisdiction. Moreover, they are in a very delicate position—in fact, effectively muzzled—if it appears that another Government department, whether or not in their own Ministry, is supporting the development, for civil servants must be polite to each other. Nor, finally, are the arguments adduced for "progress" generally confined to the logical. It is common to hear a prospective exploiter argue, first, that his scheme will be so small and peripheral that it will not detract from the amenity of the Park, and then, in the same breath, that the Park is not wild or unspoilt in any event—because it already contains developments of the sort he is proposing—and that there is thus no longer any wildness to be defended.

Much is said below about proposals for a classical form of exploitation—opencast mining in the Park—but first I must mention a few other schemes that, while they may benefit society at large rather than the purses of a few, still diminish the Park and provide excuses for its further degradation.

Through all of these examples run four threads of fallacy in current popular thought about the value and use of "undeveloped, unutilized" land.

The first is that liberty requires unlimited license to use such land in any way not directly injurious to others—for example, water-skiing on a wild lake or motor-cycling on a remote footpath. We seldom argue with enough force that some activities are by their nature completely incompatible with the purposes for which land has been reserved, and with

Those who would cut the timber, slaughter the animals as game, turn cattle loose to graze, flood the area with dams, or even open them up to real estate subdivision are fond of saying, "After all, human needs come first." But of what needs and of what human beings are we thinking? Of the material needs (or rather profits) of a few ranchers and lumbermen, or of the mental and physical health, the education and spiritual experiences, of a whole population? . . . If parks and other public lands are to be held only until someone can show that a "use" has been found for them, they will not last very much longer. If we recognize that there is more than one kind of utility and that the parks are, at the present moment, being put to the best use to be found for them, then they may last for a long time—until, perhaps, overpopulation has reached the point where the struggle for mere animal survival is so brutal that no school or theater, no concert hall or church can be permitted to "waste" the land on which it stands.

—Joseph Wood Krutch

other more numerous activities that cannot be carried out anywhere else. We must eventually decide that some recreational uses of a particular tract of land are legitimate while others, for that land at that time, are not.

Second, from the so-called democratic goal of the greatest good for the greatest number it is a short step to the proposition that any substantial crowd should be automatically allowed to use land as they wish if relatively few people object. Such an argument plainly makes it impossible to retain any genuine wilderness (which *ex hypothesi* is visited by very few) if people wish, for example, to log or ski it. (That is rather like saying that baseball is better than tennis because it has nine times as many players, and that all tennis-courts should therefore be made into baseball-diamonds.) One of the flaws in this argument is that the unique values of wilderness can be "used" in more ways than by hiking through it: many people would benefit simply by going to the edge of it and looking reflectively in, or by sitting in an armchair at home and thinking about what it means still to have wilderness, but such people would not be detected in any ordinary census of land-users.

The next fallacy is that all change is for the best, or that everything that is called progress really is. This notion ignores the Darwinian lesson's other half: that in biological evolution, most changes are in fact for the worst—so much so that they are punished by extinction. There is neither evidence nor guarantee that natural selection has made us infallible.

Lastly, these three mistakes together, when added to a debased taste for novelty and an undiscriminating acceptance of the fruits of technology, produce a monstrously one-sided reliance on cost-effectiveness arguments. It is very easy to say: Here is some land that, if used in another way that takes better advantage of our exciting new technological capabilities, would yield more profit; therefore let us so use it. Our culture, having not yet realized how much it needs wildness, or how much more it will need it, has no way of accounting for its value, or for the cost of having none. We do not yet see clearly enough that a civilized society must support some things that do not formally pay their way—music and archaeology and gardening—and that to assume that only things of known price have value is the sure path to mediocrity and barbarism. We already make some concessions to this realization: on the site of the National Gallery could doubtless be built a block of flats or offices that would yield enormous rents, and if we fail to divert the site to this use, it is because we think the Gallery has a social importance sufficient to balance its commercial unprofitability. Until we extend the same social recognition and legal protection to the wild places of the earth that we do to the seats of art and learning in our cities, seats whose lessons are supposed to reflect the lessons of nature, we shall be in no position to resist the purely economic arguments of men who, one suspects, would cheerfully build an oil-refinery in Westminster Abbey if they thought it safe and profitable.

Given that the way in which we judge proposed uses of wild land does not always protect our long-term social interests, what is the character of noncommercial developments that can benefit the nation's budget and hurt the nation's Park? how can a public benefit sought by one arm of the State destroy another benefit nominally protected by another arm?

Three kinds of schemes—water-supplying reservoirs, hydroelectric power-generating stations, and hydroelectric power-storage stations—rely on the steep, narrow valleys and the very heavy rainfall of the Park, particularly of Eryri. All these schemes are planned and executed by an authority that is under direct Government control and can therefore be expected to further the public interest more than could private companies operated for profit. I am not sure this expectation is always fulfilled.

In the administrative area that embraces much of the Park, the exploitable water supply from the many headwaters is about 500 million gallons a day, but most of it flows to the west, away from the English cities that need it, and drains too steeply to be readily impoundable. For these topographical reasons, future water-supplying developments in the Park (though not, unfortunately, in the rest of Wales) are likely to be limited. The only fairly new reservoir in the Park is a huge artificial lake, Llyn Celyn, owned and run by Liverpool Corporation. But more of Eryri's water will probably be diverted in future to the adjacent island-county of Anglesey,

formerly an isolated stronghold of ancient culture, but now becoming heavily industrialized by Shell and other consortia.

More important to the Park than water is the steadily rising demand for electricity: public water supplies now use more than twice as much of the Park's water as industry does, but only a twentieth as much as the Central Electricity Generating Board (C.E.G.B.). Electric cables scar the Park from end to end—both local distribution nets and long-distance high-tension lines—and the cost of burying them is apparently thought greater than the worth of the valleys (Maesgwm, Drws-y-coed Isaf, Llanberis Pass) that they disfigure. In Britain, as in other industrialized countries, electrical supply and demand tend to increase by a process of self-fulfilling prophecy. Once planners have decided that a certain increase of population, or of airport use, or of power consumption, will occur, they seem to do everything that will make the prediction come true, without asking whether the predicted trend is desirable or, if not, whether it can be changed. It is this sort of logic that is making us poison the earth with more and more high-level nuclear fission wastes (which we do not know how to isolate satisfactorily), even though a dead planet would obviously be bad for business; and it is this same logic that has made us reluctant to leave any river flowing without doing work for us, even though we know that tampering with watersheds always costs dearly later, in our children's time if not in ours.

Over all hung the breathless hush of evening.
One heard it circle the word like a lapping tide,
the wave-beat of the sea of beauty. . . .
We began to understand, a little less darkly,
what it may mean to inherit the earth.

—W. H. Murray

PHILIP EVANS: Detail, Llyn Mymbyr Uchaf

The C.E.G.B., which supplies power to the National Grid, already operates several hydroelectric generating stations in the Park, notably at the northeast corner of the Carneddau (where it powers an aluminium plant in Dolgarrog), at Maentwrog in Meirion, and in Cwm Dyli. (This station, built in 1906 just under the Snowdon Horseshoe, was a well-meant but largely unsuccessful early attempt at landscaped civil engineering. It is now redundant and is being dismantled, to the great relief of the landscape.) But now that the 500-megawatt nuclear power plant at Trawsfynydd in Meirion is operational, with 35 million gallons an hour of cooling water for the reactor being recycled through the vast Trawsfynydd reservoir, there is less need for power-generation than for fast-recovery power-storage, and pumped hydroelectric storage meets this need admirably.

Conventional generating plants, whether nuclear- or fossil-fueled, cannot rapidly adjust their outputs to match the fluctuating demand placed on the National Grid; but if surplus power in slack periods is used to pump water uphill from a low to a high reservoir, most of the power can then be recovered very quickly when needed by draining the water downhill again through turbines. The amount of power and the rate of recovery can be very large—the carefully landscaped station at Tanygrisiau, for example, has a height difference of a thousand feet and can pick up a third of a billion watts in less than a minute. The whole storage-and-recovery cycle cannot, of course, be perfectly efficient, and hence yields a net loss of power; but pumped storage lets generating plants all over the country run more steadily for a net economic gain, which theoretically gives the consumer cheaper electricity. The only disadvantages of pumped power-storage stations are that they often require flooding a valley for one or both of the reservoirs, that the necessary dams are intrusive, and that since the levels of both lakes fluctuate, both remain unsightly mudflats whose foreshores cannot support a normal plant population. The pumps and other buildings required for a station can be fairly well concealed either by burying or by using local stone, and the C.E.G.B., if appropriately encouraged, will do a good job of landscaping.

It is important to note that power-storage is "needed" to help the C.E.G.B.'s bookkeeping rather than to supply something we now lack. Power-storage stations do not create electricity but only store it, wasting some in the process. When to this wastage are added the stations' capital cost and running cost, it is not clear that the C.E.G.B.'s economies could not be better achieved by selling more off-peak electricity, e.g., by encouraging more strongly the use of night storage heaters. If, after considering such options more seriously than it has done, the C.E.G.B. still wanted to store power, it could think about underground compression storage, which is cheap, efficient, and largely hidden.

Undistracted by simpler solutions, the C.E.G.B. now wishes to take fuller advantage of the generating capacity of the Trawsfynydd "atomfa" and of the transmission capacity of the power-line running east from it over the Arennig range. The Board therefore hopes, though very few details have been published, to build another pumped storage facility—which, doubtless for sound technical reasons, would go into the Park. Other stations will be proposed in years to come, but only one at a time. The present new station would be concealed as much as possible, except for the inescapable effects of the varying water-levels, but it seems likely that the concealment could not be as effective as at Tanygrisiau. One possible scheme that had been rumoured—for pumping Ffynnon Lloer, a fine wild tarn under Pen yr Ole Wen and Carnedd Dafydd, in alternation with Llyn Ogwen—has apparently been abandoned, leaving three alternative sites on which further studies are now under way.

The first of these sites is Cwm Penamnen, an unspoilt wooded valley in the Glyn Lledr area above Dolwyddelan. The valley is long, steep-sided, narrow, and bottlenecked, and therefore ideal for flooding behind a dam about 170 feet high. The level of the upper lake would change over tens of yards, creating a large tract of mud-flats. The road improvements needed for the several years' construction would bring many tourists to a formerly isolated and quiet valley, much to the residents' dismay, and the village would live under the threat —no doubt more imagined than real, but no less vivid for that—of a bursting dam. The villagers also say that what little winter sunlight they now get in their narrow valley would be blocked by the dam.

Another possible site lies in lovely Cwm Croesor, between the Moelwynion and Cnicht. Of two possible schemes—a very wide 70-foot dam just above Croesor village, or a cheaper, much narrower, but very conspicuous dam over 200 feet high, sited a mile and a half up the valley—the second seems marginally the lesser evil. Yet here again, the previously undisturbed culture and the sense of security of the villagers would suffer, and compensation to the owners of the nine or so houses that would be drowned would never make up for the wider loss to the Park. The new Conservative Government's recent decision not to flood Dulas, a valley in mid-Wales, offers some hope that such social considerations may have more weight in the siting of future water projects.

The possibility of a third site, based on the use of Llynnau Marchlyn (under the north side of Elidir Fawr) as the high reservoirs and Llyn Padarn and Llyn Peris as the low, is in doubt, for the Caernarvonshire County Council, which has its own plans for Llyn Padarn, has bought some of the relevant land and has so far declined to let the C.E.G.B. do test-borings on it. The situation is complicated by the Gwynedd River Authority's alleged view that the Marchlyn lakes will eventually be used more than now as a mid-Caernarvonshire water-supply. (The possibility, once rumoured, that the Marchlynnau might be linked for pumped storage with an artificial lake in the lower part of Nant Ffrancon, a huge classic glacial valley, was probably not seriously considered by the C.E.G.B., but it revived fears of a Nant Ffrancon water project, conceived on a grand scale, that was narrowly defeated a generation ago after intense national controversy.)

The Caernarvonshire County Council's plan is to develop 270 acres around Llyn Padarn, just outside the Park, as a multi-purpose recreational park. The lake would be used for boating, swimming, and the like; there would be tenting-sites, a promenade along the shore, picnic areas, nature trails, and possibly a revived quarry-railway; the huge Dinorwic quarry, which was the mainstay of Llanberis until its recent closure, would be used as an industrial-archaeological slate museum; there might be some exploitation of the fine views of the Snowdon massif directly across the valley. All this is a logical and long-overdue development for Llanberis, a former quarry-town strategically located at the foot of Snowdon and already boasting a famous rack-and-pinion railway with an extensive history. If the County park is done in good taste, it will be welcomed in most quarters as a good exercise of initiative where it is most needed.

A development within the boundaries of the Park, and one that fewer of its residents will welcome, is the recently-approved building of over 40 chalets or somewhat larger buildings (the designs are not yet definitely settled) near one of the principal hotels in Beddgelert, a lovely village at the southern end of Eryri. It is true that chalets, if properly landscaped and designed, are less obtrusive than are permanent caravans, and may even in direct economic terms benefit a community somewhat; a planned holiday village, to be built at Bron Aber near Trawsfynydd, hopes to derive these advantages. (Chalets cannot ordinarily be built just anywhere, but most fall within the curtilage of an existing settlement, whose property values may be expected to rise if the chalets are desirable and luxurious. Cottages also pay far higher rates to the local authority than do caravan-sites.) On the other hand, the social effects of the increasing use of new and vacated houses in the Park as vacation cottages for foreigners are less desirable—some Park communities are now more than one-third "outsiders" and show a split between the outsiders and the natives.

What bothers many of the residents of Beddgelert about the chalet development is the expeditious quietness with which it was approved. A public meeting to inquire into the grant of planning permission for the chalets was in effect presented with a *fait accompli*, and with evidence that some now suspect was less than candid. Notice of a planning proposal must by law be published three weeks before the proposal is determined; but though the notice must be "published in a local newspaper circulating in the locality in which the land to which the application relates is situated," that might in practice mean a vague sentence or two buried in the back of a newspaper published, say, in Caernarvon, on the north coast, and read by only a few residents of Beddgelert, even though it can be bought there. A planning authority that feels a proposed development is minor need not give even that much notice. That a substantial body of the public were left dissatisfied with the adequacy of the notice they received shows a need for better notice; it also shows the extent to which, without any impropriety, the path of an intending developer can be smoothed in little ways by procedures whose weak requirements help (whether intentionally or not) to shield a proposal from public criticism.

AMORY LOVINS: Ffynnon Llugwy

And lonely as it is that loneliness
Will be more lonely ere it will be less—
A blanker whiteness of benighted snow
With no expression, nothing to express.
They cannot scare me with their empty spaces
Between stars—on stars where no human race is
I have it in me so much nearer home
To scare myself with my own desert places.

—ROBERT FROST
(from "Desert Places")

A similar lack of information, quite unconducive to the open discussion expected in a free society, has surrounded the most serious exploitative threat the Park has ever faced: a possibility that permission may soon be sought, and not improbably granted, for extensive opencast mining within the Park and for dredging the Park's finest estuary. A recent four-day public inquiry into applications for test-boring permission has raised more questions than it has answered; rumour and speculation are more common than fact; the persons most closely concerned prefer oral communication to written, evasive to informative, and internally inconsistent to intelligible and unambiguous. It is, in short, very hard to find out what is happening. But I have tried to collect here some of the main strands of the history, and I want to tell the tale at length, for only by learning how threats to the Park and to the idea of the Park work in practice can we hope to understand how to meet them. If my account of these threats seems more detailed and current-eventual than is usual in a book, it is because this book is in a sense a gallery, a survey of scenes and situations as they are when the photographer closes a shutter or the writer closes a sentence on what exists. To the extent that the scenes endure and the situations ease, this book will have succeeded.

"In many ponderous and ill-drafted enactments," said Sir Alan Herbert's mythical judge, Lord Wool, "our ancestors have been careful to secure to the most repellent of the King's subjects the common rights of free expression, so long as it takes the harmless form of venomous and enraging words." In the belief that the future of the Park is a matter of public interest and importance, I propose to exercise here those rights of free expression; but I have done my best to make my words not venomous and enraging, as the emotive nature of the topic urges, but fair and thought-provoking. And although the practices of the main characters make facts rare and hard to recognize, I have tried to verify the accuracy of each statement and to distinguish clearly between fact, rumour, and my own more sharply phrased opinions.

I have singled out one company, Rio Tinto Finance and Exploration Ltd. (which I shall call RTZ because it is a subsidiary of the giant Rio Tinto-Zinc Corp. Ltd., a holding company whose annual group turnover exceeds £300 million [$700 million]), simply because its activities are further advanced and easier to find out about than those of the other mining companies now also prospecting in and around the Park—Noranda Kerr (a consortium of Noranda Mines Ltd.

and Kerr Addison Mines Ltd., both of Toronto), Union Corp. Ltd. of South Africa, Geochemical Remining Co. Ltd., and possibly others.

The potential exploitation I shall describe is very controversial, and for reasons that will become clear I do not think it should be permitted to enter the Park. Yet the whole conflict would never have arisen if Britain had had any coherent national policy about mineral exploration. The laws of Britain have long presumed that the discovery and extraction of domestic minerals is in the national interest, but the laws have never made clear whether this interest is deemed sufficient to override other values for which Parliament has reserved particular tracts of land, e.g., National Parks. The test proposed by the Commission that drafted the National Parks Act—that mining in a Park must be "of proved national necessity" and "of vital national importance"—has never been made law. There is no broad land-use zoning similar to that set up for forestry in the Snowdonia National Park—no way to tell in advance whether there is a strong presumption for or against mining in a given place. This uncertainty is unfair not only to those who wonder whether their children will be able to enjoy unspoilt land, but also to the mining companies, which must take large business risks in prospecting areas that may be declared out of bounds after a heavy exploratory investment has already been made. A charitable description of present procedures would be that each case as it arises is considered locally (and perhaps nationally) on its merits; a plainer one, that until a case arises and an appointed administrator, working under a relatively haphazard procedure, has irrevocably determined the outcome, everyone must live in jeopardy. (Indeed, the jeopardy is permanent, for if one application is rejected, another may be filed at any time; and since permission, if granted, is for a use of land, and may inure to the benefit of anyone, one never knows whether one may not in future be dealing with someone other than the original applicant.)

This is not to say that British land-uses may be completely classified in advance, let alone fixed for all time; but for many areas—including, I think, National Parks—a farsighted Government would long since have expressed national intentions in clear declarations of general land-use policy. In particular, if Parliament thinks that the National Parks either can or cannot fulfil their intended functions while also being mined on a large scale, Parliament would save everyone endless trouble by saying so.

An expert witness for RTZ sought to gloss Parliament's intentions by saying at the recent public inquiry in Dolgellau: "The Minister [of Town and Country Planning], when he first introduced the Bill for the National Parks in 1949, specifically said that consideration would have to be given to working minerals in the National Park areas, if the national and local economies required it." To set the record straight, I should point out that the Minister attached more conditions than that, for the Minister went on to say: "It must be demonstrated quite clearly that the exploitation of those minerals is absolutely necessary in the public interest. It must be clear beyond all possible doubt that there is no possible alternative source of supply, and if those two conditions are satisfied then the permission must be subject to the condition that restoration takes place at the earliest possible opportunity." But there is no great scarcity of the minerals known to be in the Snowdonia National Park, but rather a comparative surplus: it is unlikely that these minerals will ever have to be mined domestically in order to avert critical shortages, except perhaps in wartime. Next, there are many excellent alternative sources with secure futures. It is true that the Mawddach estuary is Britain's only known potential source of large amounts of gold, but there are many things that are not found in Britain: there are no rubber-plantations in Britain either, but that is no reason for introducing them. Finally, the operations RTZ has in mind would be of such size as to make restoration impossible.

Yet nowadays the demand for many useful metals is increasing, the dwindling supplies are imported from faraway places at high prices, and the Exchequer is short of exportable sterling. It is natural that in such circumstances the Government should look for minerals closer to home, especially now that the price of (for example) copper is high enough that low-grade, previously uneconomic, ores can be processed profitably if on a large scale and with the most efficient modern techniques. It is natural too for some people to have assumed that the course of action that will maximize a mining company's profits is not just the best but the only possible course, and that what the private economy prefers the national economy demands.

Not only has the policy trend of recent Governments been to encourage local prospecting, but the Ministry of Technology under the recent Labour Government sought more direct incentives. MinTech was drafting, for example, proposed changes in planning law designed to thin the hedge of legalities surrounding mineral exploration. I have heard that a proposed change would have substituted the mere grant of local planning permission for the High Court order normally required to compel a landowner to permit mining on his land. It is doubtful that such legislation, if circulated more widely in draft, would have escaped modification by the opposing wishes of other Ministries, or if formally proposed, could have been passed without amendment; but that it could have been considered shows the prevailing opinion towards domestic prospecting. (Similar changes, and especially a lessening of landowners' protection against the compulsory grant of access to prospectors and extraction rights to miners, are under study by the Department of Trade and Industry in the present Government, and will be proposed in Parliament in about 1972.) It would not now be considered unusual for a mining company to write off its British exploration costs against taxes, on the grounds that the geological knowledge gained is a national asset. RTZ's statement that MinTech encouraged it to seek minerals in Snowdonia is very probably true, at least with regard to the Mawddach estuary.

When challenged recently by articulate journalists who oppose its prospecting and potential mining in the Park, RTZ has taken the righteously aggrieved position of a boy who, when caught raiding the candy-jar, says his mother told him to. RTZ thinks it is ungrateful for people who have, through their Government, encouraged it to prospect in the Park to complain about the possible consequences—especially since the extraction of a strategic metal such as copper from the Park would allegedly increase Britain's self-sufficiency and prosperity, ends doubtless desired by every patriotic Briton.

Indeed, RTZ finds all publicity about its actions in the Park painful, and all speculation about its intentions distressing; so I fear that it will be pained and distressed by this book. For I do not agree that what is good for RTZ is good for Britain. On the contrary, I suspect, having studied the evidence that follows, that what is good for RTZ is very likely to be bad for Britain, in ways less obvious and more important than balance-of-payments accounts would show.

Simply put, my arguments are: mineral extraction of the sort RTZ contemplates is entirely and unalterably incompatible with the purposes of a National Park, as Parliament has declared those purposes; most of Britain's nonferrous metal ores are in her National Parks or in other wild country of equal beauty; in particular, the 300-square-mile Harlech Dome of Snowdonia is probably the greatest mineral-storehouse in Britain; the extraction of these minerals is already profitable and will become steadily more so; an easily calculable (and more easily inflatable) benefit must be balanced against a less tangible loss; Britain can have either a prosperous mining industry or a system of National Parks, but not both forever. Either the miners or the Parks, or both in compromise, must eventually give up some of their potential.

It has been said with some wry truth that the admission of mining to the Snowdonia National Park would not by itself constitute a watershed for National Park policy, because there is no such policy; but at least if Snowdonia is not thought by the British people to be worth saving from mining, no National Park is worth it, and Parliament was wrong in implying that the scenic value of the National Parks is so important as to override any other possible use to which the land might be put. I would prefer to put the question to Parliament, for I think, with Herbert's Lord Mildew, that "if Parliament does not mean what it says it must say so." The National Parks Act is, despite appearances, still law, and it is hard to see how its objects (quoted at the beginning of this section) could be furthered by RTZ's projected exploitation.

I must point out at once that RTZ has not yet formally proposed any dredging or mining in the Park, but has carefully limited its written public statements to the details of the preliminary studies needed to decide whether any extraction could profitably take place. Why, RTZ asks, should we object to a few holes in the ground, holes that will advance the interests of geological science and that may well show nothing of value to miners?

Since minerals can be mined only where they are found, the answer depends on whether we think there are any circumstances in which we would be prepared to consider eventual large-scale mining in the Park. If we entertain such a thought, we are saying that everything, even the Park, has its price. A nation in which everything has its price will soon have few priceless things left, for if each asset and man and principle has a price, it is equally true that RTZ has the money, and if it is not RTZ it will be someone else. If the minerals were not in the Park, we should get on very well without them; but if we let RTZ find out they are there, we must consider RTZ's bid, and balance conflicting expressions of national interest that are very hard to compare.

Permitting prospecting in the Park is thus admitting the thin edge of the wedge, in a more insidiously dangerous way than is at first apparent. If geological studies are allowed to substitute firm, plump numbers (such as fifty million pounds) for nebulous guesses, and to substitute what appears to be a single small operation—local, brief, and hidden—for an immense looming threat, it is very likely that the bait will be taken, without a thought that a Park held permanently in trust for the nation under the enduring power of law has suddenly become a Park temporarily existing by the tenuous and capricious grace of Ministerial discretion. It seems extraordinary that Parliament should first set aside a National Park and then allow a Minister to authorize massive industrialization there, but such seems to be the law. At the recent public inquiry, the Merioneth Planning Officer suggested the possible outcome when he said that RTZ should not be allowed to do test-borings in the Park. RTZ's counsel cross-examined him:

"Q. Because if we found a lot of gold or a lot of copper, that might show that the proper planning decision then would be to allow such mining to take place?

"A. I do not think such a decision could ever be a proper planning decision. It might influence somebody to give consent in spite of the proper planning decision. . . . I do not think we would trust anyone with a large amount of gold."

PHILIP EVANS: Conway Falls

Even if exploration showed that the ores were too poor to be worth mining, the Park would have no more than a reprieve, for today's poor ores will eventually be considered rich. The knowledge that the Park is living on borrowed time would be a sword of Damocles over the heads of its residents and planners; prospecting has already cast a generation-long planning blight over the Park. Mining would be repeatedly proposed, with increasingly cogent arguments, until it was allowed. Nor would short-range appraisals of the worth of mining schemes be likely to consider that profitable extractive industries are rarely satisfied with one windfall when another is there for the taking; or that copper-mining becomes even more profitable if local smelters are installed (bringing ecological havoc with them); or that if smelters are not installed, vast tonnages of rock must be transported to, say, Swansea, an impossible task without a new rail line, highway, or harbour. The lesson learned in the National Parks of the United States, very bitterly and almost too late, is that if you once let the technological vultures nibble at a Park, they will flock and feast in the most modern way until nothing is left— and as they gorge themselves they will assure you that it doesn't hurt a bit and is really for your own good.

If there were such a national emergency that Britain's survival depended on her finding local mineral reserves, it would be easier to argue that the Park must be sacrificed to overwhelming necessity. But there is no such emergency now; nor do the other industrialized countries of western Europe, which rely on the same sources of minerals and pay the same prices, seem worried. If a national crisis arose, so grave as to make the value of a Park a trivial consideration, the minerals, if left undisturbed now, would still be there. But that the value of the Park is not trivial but great and increasing was recognized by Parliament in the Countryside Act, 1968.

Ironically, not only are present world supplies of copper adequate, but there is a glut on the market. The plummeting price of copper today is due partly to reaction against earlier inflated prices, partly to reduced American and Japanese orders, but mostly to the great success of RTZ and other companies in exploiting low-grade ores throughout the world, especially in New Guinea and southern Africa. There is no shortage of copper now, nor will there be soon. But though immediate exploitation of British ores would be unnecessary and absurd, RTZ is proceeding to sew up future UK mining options in order to protect its competitive position two or three decades hence, when RTZ assumes the world demand for copper will have increased sharply—perhaps a dubious assumption if more copper is recycled (an enterprise in which RTZ has shown little interest). Proceeding on the assumption of vast future growth, RTZ wishes to reserve to itself the right to mine in Snowdonia and other British wildlands. RTZ has just been licensed to prospect in 175 square miles of Co. Down and Co. Tyrone in Northern Ireland—a lovely area that includes the Mountains of Mourne—and other com-

panies are exploring larger tracts in the same area. Most wild regions of Britain, including the Scottish Highlands and the Lake District, are reportedly being explored by many companies seeking (and finding) everything from tungsten to uranium.

The precedent for substantial new mining in British National Parks has already been set. RTZ recently found, in the North York Moors National Park, Britain's first domestic deposit of potash, and has been authorized to extract it through a series of small but visually intrusive solute-pumping stations scattered along a pretty section of coastline. The stations are to produce both the desired product, which is to be hauled away, and waste brine, which is to be pumped out to sea with ecological effects that are still unclear. Two other companies have also been authorized to mine the potash, though they, like RTZ, are hesitating to do so because the market has turned out to be smaller than they had hoped. That there is a limit to encroachments in that particular Park was recently and belatedly shown when the Minister followed the advice of the Park Planning Committee in denying permission to explore there for gas and oil.

I do not see how large-scale extraction of minerals in the Snowdonia National Park could be done in a way compatible with the Park's proper functions. (Very small underground projects have always been acceptable in the Park, and still are.) If profit is to be had from low-grade ores, enormous volumes of ore must be processed by efficient large-scale machinery. RTZ has spoken reassuringly about the ways in which an opencast mine, for example, can be "cosmeticized" with modern landscaping techniques. But in the sense in which cosmeticization is meant to be taken, I think it is untrue and impossible.

It is certainly feasible to hide an open pit or working behind "artificial mountains"—heaps of tailings 600 feet high—but it is not clear how this would beautify the mine, nor that a National Park should be a place in which you create the hideous and then hide it with the ugly, nor that the huge volumes of material removed from an RTZ working would or could be replaced at an acceptable cost or made to support vegetation. (Copper concentrations less than one part per million arrest root development in many plants.) I have seen no evidence that it is possible either to conceal or to restore a pit covering several hundred acres: all the available evidence suggests it is not, in that such remedial cosmetic operations can at best be only marginally successful. The basic scars of opencast mining are ugly, prominent, and permanent. RTZ has privately proposed, therefore, not to fill in its opencast workings, but to flood them, creating large "recreational" lakes or hydroelectric reservoirs. I do not understand where the needed water will come from, how it can be kept there without serious geological repercussions, or how any plants or animals can live in water so full of mineral salts. I am sure that whatever artists' impressions RTZ may produce, such a lake, if it could be built, would be far from an improvement on the present scenery. It would only be a modern, consummately skilful, largely unsuccessful attempt to conceal devastation—perhaps at public expense via an "amenity grant."

Lord Byers, who is both Director of Exploration for RTZ and the leader of the Liberal Party in the House of Lords, recently wrote in the *New Scientist:* "RTZ policy is crystal clear. We are conservationists. We are also miners. We believe that by harnessing the finest brains in the conservation field, ecologists, landscape architects, chemical and construction engineers together with our own geologists, mining engineers and metallurgists, we can show that natural beauty and mining can go hand in hand but at a cost. If they cannot go hand in hand or the cost is too great to show a profitable venture, we will not undertake it. It is a simple and an honest policy." If Lord Byers allows the conservationist in him to take precedence over the miner—a move his employers might dislike—I am sure he will agree with me that RTZ's venture into the Park is a mistake, for to maintain an opencast mine or dredging operation of the necessary size and to try to retain only a very moderate standard of contrived beauty where natural beauty was would strain even RTZ's resources. As matters stand, neither RTZ's past conduct in the Park nor the character of its mines elsewhere gives me any confidence that the Park's interests would be well served by reliance on RTZ's good-will or conservationist instincts—or on the recent statement of its Chairman, Sir Val Duncan, that RTZ "has always accepted that the preservation of amenity is of prime importance." The same goes for other companies, including Noranda Kerr, whose spokesman has reportedly said, "We're really only at the stage at which a geologist bangs at a bit of rock with a hammer. We have the conservation of the environment at the forefront of our minds." I think it is unsafe to allow mining in the Park "with suitable safeguards"; for as we shall see, if agreed standards were sufficiently high not to make an intolerable mess of the Park, they could not be enforced, since suitable rehabilitation of the amount of desert that would be created would be a physical impossibility. Thus I doubt that Lord Byers's admirable sentiments bear the same meaning to him that they do to conservationists outside the mining industry. When he writes about conservation, the right catch-words come out, but there is disturbingly little evidence that they express the right thoughts.

I do not think it is fair to view RTZ as a group of cynical despoilers who calculate just how much amenity they must propose, against their principles, in order to get their projects approved. If they were men of that sort they would be easier to combat. The attitude of RTZ officials is in fact just the opposite (and in a sense all the more evil): they sincerely believe themselves to be conservationists; they feel honestly entitled to ask, like Sir Toby Belch, "Am not I consanguineous?"; they do, amazingly, think that turning the Mawddach estuary into a freshwater lake lined with marinas would be a public good that ought to make everyone happy. This is such a gross misconception of what conservation means that I am not sure where to begin their re-education, for they simply do not see in land the same values that a real conservationist does, and they do not realize that it is both easier and more in the public interest to extract copper from scrap-metal than from low-grade ores mined in wild places. But at least there is no harm trying to convince RTZ's policy-makers that it is possible for someone to prefer the Mawddach in its present unimproved state without his being (as they visualize the typical pro-Park fanatic to be) committed to "fossilizing" the Park—leaving it exactly as it is for all time, letting nobody but himself enter, and selfishly keeping the residents from making a decent living.

People often say that RTZ's potentially huge business in the Park would have a strong effect on the local economy. I think this is true, but perhaps in a different way from the speakers' intention. I shall discuss the economic consequences of mining below, after setting out just what RTZ seems to have in mind.

RTZ has two main prospects in the Park: first, the possibility of dredging for alluvial gold in the Mawddach estuary; second, the less vigorously opposed and ultimately perhaps more alarming possibility of opencast mining for copper in the wooded hills near Dolgellau. Although these are the only two specific schemes I shall describe, and both are in west-central Meirion, it is important to remember that prospectors seeking gold, copper, zinc, manganese, lead, silver, and other minerals are now swarming all over the Park, even conducting tests on the Snowdon massif itself. Most of the farmers in the central part of the Park have been approached by various companies outbidding each other for prospecting rights, some of them offering contracts that I should advise anyone not to sign at any price. The offers are, on the local scale, generous; a hill-farmer, for example, is quoted in the press as saying he was offered £150 ($360) for three years' prospecting rights on his fairly small holding. In Gwynedd, and for the mere right to prospect, that is a tempting offer, unlikely to be declined—especially when backed by a threat of compulsory access or purchase. Most of the available prospecting and mining rights in the Park are now bought by companies that are waiting to see how RTZ succeeds. The spokesman for one of these firms is quoted in the *Observer* as saying: "[RTZ's] application is *the* test-case for mineral mining in Britain, and particularly for areas which have tourist interests, such as Snowdonia."

Here, then, is a short account of RTZ's two sites of interest within the Park, beginning with the Mawddach estuary. This is a case-history, and it is extrapolable. If we do not learn quickly what it has to teach us, it will be an archetype for the destruction of the National Parks of Britain—in the name of the national interest and by the leave of national lack of interest.

That land is a community is the basic concept of ecology,
but that land is to be loved and respected is an extension of ethics.
That land yields a cultural harvest is a fact long known
but latterly often forgotten.

—ALDO LEOPOLD

5. Miners

THE MAWDDACH estuary is a large area of alluvial plain and tidal flats where Afon [river] Mawddach comes down to the Sea. The estuary runs westward from Dolgellau, the inland seat of Merioneth, to the coast at Barmouth, a distance of about seven miles, and is entirely within the National Park except for a small area near Barmouth.

The estuary has long been famous as one of the most beautiful in the world. The delicate and sinuous tracery of its meandering channels through the flats is contrasted with the wild grandeur of the Cader Idris massif immediately to the south and the ruggedness of the Rhinog range to the north. It is possible to walk the length of the estuary along the relatively peaceful hills overlooking it, enjoying the remarkable play of light and shadow over the colourful flats, and observing the variety of birds and other wildlife that the estuary supports.

Afon Mawddach drains a large watershed that includes most of the old gold-mining belt of Meirion, and the estuary probably contains alluvial gold washed down from the hills. The deepest-lying sediments, closest to the bedrock, would contain the most gold. RTZ has already made resistivity and seismic studies to try to find the depth of the alluvial sediments, but these measurements are imprecise without calibration by test-borings. Such borings would reveal both how much of the estuarine floor of bedrock is within the depth-limit of modern dredging techniques, and how much gold there is in various places; hence whether dredging would be profitable.

It is common ground that each of the proposed test-borings, while it would annoy some residents, would probably have only slight and transient effects on the estuary's ecology and scenery. But the cumulative nuisance and damage would be substantial if there were very many holes. An indefinite number of holes, six or eight inches in diameter and up to 300 feet deep, would be drilled within a 1775-acre tract in or around the estuary, each hole taking a crew of four to six men about a week or ten days to make with a small diesel rig on a derrick about 30 feet high. But the number, size, and working schedules of the rig(s) needed could not be specified until the subcontractor had actually begun work; nor would the number of holes be limited unless the Secretary of State for Wales cared to set a limit, for though RTZ talked, in oral evidence at the Dolgellau inquiry, about drilling from five to twelve holes, the formal application contained no such limit. If the Secretary did limit the present drilling, a favourable result from it would lead to an application for more; RTZ's written proposal mentions "the initial programme" (taking about two or three months) and leaves open the question of possible further drilling. Finally, whatever the number and nature of the holes drilled, the drilling would intrude on the peace of the landscape, and if permitted would be an irresistible precedent for allowing test-boring anywhere in the Park.

Extraction of the alluvial gold would inevitably be far more harmful than test-boring. Estuaries are poorly understood but are known to have a peculiarly delicate drainage-pattern and ecology, hard to generalize about because each estuary has unique quirks of behaviour. Yet a few details of what will happen if the Mawddach is dredged have already become clear.

The dredging would reportedly be carried out by at least one dredger, roughly 320 by 80 by 80 feet in size and guided by cables strung across the channel; there might be several such dredgers. Dredging would take about 15 years, possibly as long as 30. Either of two obvious techniques might be used for floating the dredger(s): a gravel barrage could block the mouth of the estuary, alongside an existing railway bridge, or the dredger(s) could progress from place to place by digging a series of lagoons. The former procedure would probably be very expensive, produce a high risk of flooding unless many dams were built upstream, and cause massive silting of the estuary—an effect that has already done much harm since the railway bridge was built, although the bridge has reduced the flood-scouring and flow-rate of the estuary far less than a barrage would. A barrage would eventually turn the estuary into one big mud-flat. Using the less expensive lagoon system, on the other hand, would ruin the present flow-patterns of the estuary in a more localized way but with long-range effects potentially as severe, for even a small change in flow at one point in an estuary has consequences far-reaching in time and space, so delicately is the drainage balanced. Despite RTZ's denials that a barrage scheme is being considered, I am reliably informed that it is in fact the method most likely to be proposed.

Whichever of the two methods were used, the suspended silt produced by dredging would for its duration spoil the angling (largely for migratory fish) in the estuary—an activity that yields close to £40,000 a year to the landowners. The excretion of an immense volume of dredging waste ("tailings") would produce many heaps of mud dotted about the estuary. These hillocks might well subside after an unknown time, but there is no sound evidence on the point.

The long-term ecological effects of dredging are also unknown. Nobody can say, for example, whether the changes in dissolved mineral-salt concentrations arising from dredging would harm the estuarine plants or wildlife. The wild birds in the estuary would almost certainly go away and salmon would probably not run ladders in a barrage. RTZ is not qualified to consider such matters, for it has had only very limited experience of dredging, gained in several years of it off the Malayan coast, and no experience at all of estuarine dredging.

RTZ has taken general advice from [unnamed] consultants on the feasibility—not necessarily the possible ecological consequences—of dredging, but has undertaken no formal studies. When asked whether the estuarine character would be altered by dredging of the sort contemplated, RTZ's main representative at the public inquiry admitted that it would, although he would not concede that the change would be for the worse.

Collecting all the available clues to RTZ's possible intentions in the Mawddach, I suspect the estuary would be not restored (which of course would be impossible) but "improved" after being barred, flooded, and dredged. This "improvement" would take whichever of two forms seemed politically more expedient: either confining the river to a network of drainage channels and draining the flats completely for agriculture—the project could then be called "land reclamation" or "flood control"—or deep-dredging the estuary into a "recreational" freshwater reservoir or lake, which would presumably have to be re-dredged periodically to remove silt to a depth suitable for boating. Either of these proposals, backed by the prospect of a new coastal trunk road along the barrage, and perhaps of a new harbour at Barmouth, would have many backers. RTZ would sincerely view such schemes as improvements on the landscape, and would not see the analogy suggested by Professor Allen when he said, "So far as I know, Picasso was never invited to overpaint a Rembrandt." (I am sure Professor Allen meant no disrespect to Picasso.)

Under British law, any test-boring for mineral exploration constitutes development requiring prior permission from the local planning authorities. There is no case-law so specifying, perhaps because the relevant statute is itself very clear. Section 12.1 of the Town and Country Planning Act, 1962, provides, with certain stated exceptions that are irrelevant here, that "'development' . . . means the carrying out of building, engineering, mining or other operations in on, over, or under land, or the making of any material change in the use of any buildings or other land." It seems clear to all the officials concerned—for example, the Department of the Environment, the Welsh Office, and the Merioneth County Council—that exploratory drilling falls squarely within this definition. The exemption from planning rules that is afforded to temporary changes of land-use (for periods shorter than four weeks) does not apply to mineral operations.

RTZ, however, seems to find room for doubt, and says it has been advised that its proposed drilling in the Mawddach does not in law require planning permission. Nonetheless, since the landowners (the Crown Estates Commissioners) have expressed the opposite opinion, RTZ has applied for such permission, giving meanwhile the impression that this application is a courtesy rather than a necessity.

The question whether planning permission is needed for test-boring is very important, for on this point hinges whether or not it is fair to view in a most unfavourable light RTZ's past activities at its other site of interest in the Park.

The site is the Capel Hermon area of Coed-y-brenin, a large forest in the hills near Dolgellau. The tenant of the land is the Forestry Commission, but the ground landlord has retained the mineral rights and has given RTZ permission to prospect. RTZ's only dealing with the Commission has been an access agreement to make good any damage done to roads, paths, etc.

In the dense and well-concealed depths of Coed-y-brenin (The King's Wood), RTZ has already drilled four dozen holes, some of them apparently much deeper than those proposed for the Mawddach. (Some of the holes are even said by local residents to be about 1000 feet deep, but RTZ has partly denied this.) The odd feature of this drilling is that unlike that proposed for the Mawddach, it has all been done without benefit of planning permission, and in an air of secrecy. RTZ began prospecting in Coed-y-brenin in May 1968 and test-boring in January 1969, but the Merioneth County Council, which should by law have been approached first for a grant of planning permission for the drilling, was not officially informed of its existence until December 1969.

Lord Byers has written that RTZ "has kept the [county] officials apprised of its activities from the beginning." It is not clear what this means. The facts seem to be that RTZ did tell several local people about the drilling within a few months of its being started, but these people were not the ones to whom the information was legally due, and were in any event informed in confidence—a reasonable-sounding course for a company that wanted to obtain local exploration options before widespread publicity raised the prices. Certain County officials got wind of the drilling unofficially in June 1969 through what was probably a breach of confidence by a third party, and sent to the woods a representative who was told by the men at a drilling rig that they would be through working next week. They meant through at that site, but he thought they meant through for good, and when they were still drilling six months later the County Council arranged a meeting with RTZ's representatives.

At this meeting, in January 1970, RTZ was told that drilling of the sort being carried on required a grant of planning permission. Applications for such permission were accordingly filed with the Council at the end of April 1970; but both before and after this filing, the drilling continued at a quickening pace, with some of the drill-rigs running day and night. At the suggestion, made a month later, of the County Planning Officer, the applications for test-boring both in Coed-y-brenin and in the Mawddach were "called in" by the Secretary of State for Wales in mid-July; this is a procedure under which a planning issue of national importance is determined personally by a civil servant with Ministerial responsibilities rather than decided on the local level. A public inquiry into the merits of the test-boring applications for both sites was announced on 23 October 1970 and held in a small hall in Dolgellau on 15-18 December. Such an inquiry is the normal procedure for gathering evidence submitted by the parties concerned and by the public; an Inspector, acting under instructions from the Minister, presides over the inquiry, then writes a report for the Minister in which he summarizes the arguments adduced by all those who submit evidence and makes his own recommendations. The Minister, after deliberating, then decides the issue in his absolute discretion, and announces his binding decision—an event expected in the late spring of 1971.

Several circumstances of this chronology are bound to disappoint those concerned with the future of the Park. First, the Forestry Commission was not, of course, legally obliged to report to the County authorities the extensive drilling being done on the land of which it was a tenant; nevertheless it is unfortunate that the Commission did not gratuitously do so anyway, since that would have prevented uncharitable persons from entertaining the doubtless unworthy suspicion that the Commission's silence may have been motivated by the enormous benefits, direct and indirect, that it and the ground landlord would receive if the land-use were in future partly changed from forestry to mining. I think the Commission would have been wiser, however narrow its strict legal duties, to bend over backwards to avoid giving any grounds for thinking that there may have been wheels within wheels here. But perhaps the Commission did not speculate about the legality of the drilling, or felt that silence was the best way to fulfil its public duty of making the best possible profit from the land of which it is a tenant.

Likewise, the County Council cannot be said to have turned a blind eye to drilling, but neither can it be said to have enforced the law with notable vigour and despatch. However little and late the official information of violations may have come to the attention of the Council, the fact remains that drilling in Coed-y-brenin went on, in violation of planning law, from January 1969 until at least 6 November 1970, even though RTZ was officially informed by the Council in January 1970 that the law required permission for drilling. The drilling actually stopped only when the Welsh Office, well after it had called in the application (but before the inquiry), told RTZ to stop. At about that time, widespread public indignation was being aroused by press reports and by Jon Tinker's extensive revelations in the *New Scientist* of 12 November.

The County Council says that it expected, for reasons that are not at all clear, to be able to resolve promptly the questions raised by the applications of April 1970—so promptly that it took no steps to halt the drilling. The Council never formally rejected RTZ's applications, but passed them on to higher authority at the first opportunity, thus depriving itself of the chance to issue an enforcement order against the continuing illegal drilling before the calling in of the applications made

the whole affair *sub judice*. For a very long time, the Council pursued its rather ponderous inquiries through the proper official channels without taking forcible action to stop an important and continuous violation of a law that the Council is charged with administering. Perhaps I am expecting an unreasonably intemperate haste inconsistent with the dignity of government, but while I certainly do not ascribe to the Council any impropriety or delaying tactics, I still think its powers could have been used far more decisively. The Council's courage in eventually opposing the applications is commendable, but had the Council acted sooner, the damage would not have been done. Even if the Council intended (as it probably did at first) to approve the drilling, I think it ought to have stopped the drilling during discussions; it is absurd to decide whether to give someone permission to do what he is already doing without it.

The drilling of 48 holes in Coed-y-brenin, sometimes round the clock and seven days a week, caused great annoyance to many residents. At one extreme, a farmer complained that when RTZ's first bore-hole on his land made a mess, he withdrew his consent for more, whereupon RTZ drilled seven holes right along his boundary, including one hole within 50 yards of his front door. That is much too close for comfort. RTZ claims that its diesel rigs make no more noise than a farm-tractor. That may be true of the engine alone, but apparently the drill-bit and the driving-gear whine loudly, and the men must also do a lot of hammering on the casings; and tractors do not run for hours at a time, nor at night. It is unclear how many visitors to the forest were annoyed by the drilling; RTZ hired a public-opinion-surveying firm to find out, and the withholding of evidence of the poll from the public inquiry may suggest to the suspicious that the results did not favour RTZ's case.

RTZ's future course near Capel Hermon is uncertain, but it seems likely that if the Secretary of State for Wales grants drilling permission, the first phase of continuing exploration on the 2475-acre tract will take from four to twelve drilling-rigs about a year to complete. (As in the Mawddach scheme, RTZ has limited the number of holes proposed in its oral evidence, which is not binding, but has set no limit in its written application, which is.) If it then appeared to RTZ that the prospects for profitable copper-mining in the area were good, simultaneous applications would be filed immediately, about the end of spring 1972, both for intensive exploration (costing roughly £2 million) and for subsequent extraction, which might in practice be postponed for many years. The Mawddach scheme might take about the same time as the Coed-y-brenin scheme to go before the final inquiry, since although the geology is probably simpler, no drilling has yet been done.

I find it hard to avoid concluding that RTZ drilled without permission in Coed-y-brenin not out of a mistake as to the law but because it seemed possible to get away with it, while any test-boring in the open country of the Mawddach would be obvious at once. One cannot argue that the Coed-y-brenin drilling is less likely than the proposed Mawddach drilling to need planning permission, since the former has been both deeper and more extensive than the latter.

RTZ claims to have been advised that exploratory drilling does not need planning permission. It is hard to believe that this claim has substance, whatever the source of the alleged advice. Certainly such advice could not have come from the county or national Governments, which would have said the opposite. Jon Tinker quotes Lord Byers as attributing the advice to MinTech, but I understand that that Ministry's successor (the Department of Trade and Industry) has since denied, in a letter to Mr. Tinker, that MinTech gave such advice—at least officially. (It is also implausible both that MinTech would have offered advice on a matter plainly within the jurisdiction of the Welsh Office, and that MinTech could have been so ignorant of the mineral-exploration laws it was working to change.) Perhaps RTZ obtained its advice from its expert and highly paid legal staff, but if so it is hard to see either why the official view of the law differs or why RTZ bothered in the end to apply forthwith for permission rather than simply contesting the Government's position in court—thus perhaps removing the need for many proposed changes in exploration law. Finally, there is no doubt that RTZ continued drilling for nearly a year after being officially told that unapproved drilling is illegal. If RTZ seriously thought this view of the law was wrong, I think it would have been more consistent with "a simple and an honest policy" for RTZ to seek judicial construction of the allegedly unclear statute.

Lord Byers has written: "Legal advice taken by RTZ indicates that the initial shallow scout drilling with small rigs does not require planning permission, but concentrated and deeper drilling does do so." Mr. N. Greenwood, writing to the *New Scientist* (where Lord Byers's remark appeared), points out that if Lord Byers is correct, his company seems to have rejected both parts of the advice, since RTZ did not apply (until forced to) for permission for the undoubtedly deep and concentrated drilling it has been carrying on in Coed-y-brenin, but did seek permission in advance for the comparatively diffuse and shallow drilling in the Mawddach. RTZ's geologist in charge of the former operation further clouded Lord Byers's statement by saying at the inquiry that his crews had carried out not only scout drilling but also prospect drilling, a more advanced phase.

The exact form that copper-mining near Dolgellau might take if the test-borings showed promising deposits is rather hypothetical, both because RTZ's technical witnesses at the inquiry declined to testify on such speculative matters and because Lord Byers has been quoted as giving different numbers to different people. The only safe generalizations at this point are that there would be about two to four opencast sites, each probably about 200 acres in size and several hundred feet deep (i.e., having a volume corresponding to about 250 million tons of rock); that the total area involved would be of order one square mile or a bit more, and the total investment well over £40 million; that the amount of rock extracted would be very large, probably tens of millions of tons a year, since the average copper concentration is thought to be less than 1 per cent; that present transport could not handle such a load, even with considerable on-site pre-processing; and that the approval of a proposal for such mining would lead to many similar applications from other companies and for other sites throughout most of the Park and in other Parks. Even the approval of the test-boring applications will trigger a flood of others from companies that view RTZ's present effort as a test-case.

moon newly minted
air bitter copper tasting
white stoop-shouldered stones

AMORY LOVINS: *Stream detail, Cwm Lloer*

Men push farther and farther in their search for "resources"
to be exploited, even for more mere space to occupy.
Increasingly they tend to think of the terrestrial globe as *their* earth.
They never doubt their right to deal with it as they think fit—
and what they think fit usually involves the destruction of what
nature has thought fit during many millions of years. . . .

The wisest, the most enlightened, the most remotely
long-seeing exploitation of resources is not enough,
for the simple reason that the whole concept of exploitation
is so false and so limited that in the end it will defeat itself
and the earth will have been plundered no matter how scientifically
and far-seeingly the plundering has been done.

—Joseph Wood Krutch

Coed-y-brenin is a man-made landscape in the sense that its trees were planted, but it is also a living landscape. It cannot be called an outstandingly spectacular part of the Park, but neither can every part of Chartres Cathedral be said to be outstanding relative to the rest of it. The Forestry Commission, in its pamphlet, calls Coed-y-brenin "a mountain forest of superlative beauty." Coed-y-brenin supports a characteristic flora and fauna in a relatively undisturbed state—including at least 350 species of flowering plants, and 20 of the 27 British mammals. It is a very dense mosaic of habitats, important as a regenerative centre for bird populations. Its remarkable combination of wooded hills and river-gorge is fairly isolated from the main tourist routes; it is not, as the Mawddach is, a famous beauty-spot heavily patronized by foreigners. For that reason, it is possible that permission for further exploration may be granted for Coed-y-brenin but not for the Mawddach. (RTZ is prepared to accept such a decision; it cares more about the huge deposits of inland copper than about the relatively small amount—say one or two million pounds' worth—of alluvial gold.) This partial permission is a politically attractive course, but would be very dangerous to the Park.

The County Planning Officer for Merioneth has made clear that whether or not RTZ gives an offered assurance that a grant of permission for exploration would not be used to support a possible later request for mining permission, "a successful drilling operation carried out with the Secretary of State's consent will set the stage for large scale open-cast mining not only here but also in other parts of the National Park. Furthermore it will establish that the National Parks and the protection supposedly afforded to them by the National Parks Act . . . [have] no real significance in the mind of the Secretary of State. This could only mean the practical abandonment of the National Park concept."

This view is reinforced by Jon Tinker's quotation of Lord Byers as telling him, "I would loathe to see opencast mining in all [ten of] our national parks, but in two or three it would be OK." Lord Byers has since written that this statement "is a fabrication and at odds with the views I hold. While I believe that, dependent on the topography and the type of ore body, it would be possible to reconcile the preservation of a very high standard of amenity with mining operation, trying to quantify would be impossible." He has not responded to Mr. Tinker's reply: "In how many national parks, then, *would* he like to see opencast mining?"

The Merioneth Planning Officer has also pointed out ". . . that although the applications were for drilling only they would not be made unless the Company hoped to extract any minerals found whose extraction was profitable. In the event that preliminary drilling disclosed the presence of minerals in quantities and places from which it was profitable to extract them, . . . supplementary applications would be made for more intensive drilling and for . . . extraction. . . .

[The Park] Joint Advisory Committee and the [Merioneth County Council Park] Planning Committee took the view that the applications for exploration and extraction were merely different stages of one development and inextricably joined. . . . In the event of the exploration proving that there were minerals there which were profitable[,] it would be, regardless of any undertaking given by the applicants, more difficult to resist applications to exploit and extract. . . ." In other words, full mining permission is most difficult to refuse if approached—as RTZ is doing—by discreet and discrete stages of creeping.

The view that acceptance of proposals for exploratory drilling implies a willingness at least to consider possible later proposals for extraction may seem obviously valid, but has been strongly resisted by RTZ, which has on the contrary tried to give the impression that it is exploring out of academic interest, with very long odds against any commercial success. RTZ accordingly took great pains to narrow the scope of the public inquiry from general policy questions about the consequences of allowing drilling to a strict consideration of the actual applications, entirely divorced from any possible later applications. Thus from the start the inquiry was kept from coming to grips with the real issues at stake—because RTZ chose, for obvious reasons, not to discuss them. Yet witnesses in favour of RTZ adduced arguments on the same topics—e.g., employment resulting from eventual mining—that objectors were unable to pursue against RTZ, which thus had the best of both worlds.

The brilliant presentation made by Queen's Counsel retained by RTZ rationalized the company's dodging of the development issues. Following a non-binding precedent set in RTZ's successful pursuit of permission to mine potash in the North York Moors National Park, and apparently following the mandate of a closed-doors procedural conference held in the Welsh Office on 19 October, the Inspector began the inquiry by saying that he would limit its terms of reference to the merits of the test-boring applications *per se*. When the Merioneth County Council's advocate pointed out that the Secretary of State for Wales would hardly have called in the applications as a matter "of national importance and interest" if he thought no more was involved than a few holes in the ground, and that the Inspector would hardly be sitting with an expert geologist and a mining assessor if these subjects were not to be discussed, the Inspector had to concede that he would accept and report any testimony offered on the broader implications of the test-boring proposals, but he could not guarantee that the Secretary would take any notice of it. But no evidence was sought on land-use policy or on long-term planning implications, and thus the Inspector did not make a reasonable effort to inform himself (and the Secretary) on the matters RTZ did not consider relevant to its applications— matters which all the objectors were interested in.

Since there seemed to be doubt about how broad the

Secretary wanted the inquiry's terms of reference to be, the representative of the Ramblers' Association suggested an adjournment so that the Secretary's intentions could be ascertained. RTZ's counsel made this remarkable comment: "If we [RTZ] are right, it will be quite wrong that the decision on this inquiry should be delayed because people want to get a decision from the Secretary of State about matters which, on this view of the matter, are irrelevant at this stage."—and the inquiry continued.

The actual conduct of the inquiry, although it accorded with the legally prescribed forms, left little room for serious objection to RTZ's proposals. RTZ sent only two technical representatives, men clearly very experienced in mineral extraction (except by dredging); but when asked about any matter outside the narrow scope of the test-boring applications, they declined to answer, saying the subject was outside their competence or that they had not been instructed on it, and

dismissing any matters more than a few months in the future as wild speculation. (Ecological questions were obviously and regrettably outside their competence; but on details of, for example, opencast mining, some spectators gathered that they had indeed been instructed—to say nothing.) Attempts to find out RTZ's longer-range plans were thus continually frustrated by a lack of information, for which the inquiry's limited terms of reference left no remedy. Furthermore, few of the people present had the technical background to question RTZ's schemes, and the lack of a public-address system left much of the audience unable to hear the testimony. The inquiry was left to grapple with the complex issues of employment, trade, and public investment without the benefit of evidence from the Government Departments specializing in such questions, for of course they had not been consulted. The Inspector seemed unfamiliar both with the area (which he later went to inspect) and with Welsh.

PHILIP EVANS: Icicles, Cwm-glas-mawr

The finest workers in stone are not copper or steel tools,
but the gentle touches of air and water
working at their leisure with a liberal allowance of time.
—THOREAU

Every raincloud, however fleeting, leaves its mark,
not only on trees and flowers whose pulses are quickened,
and on the replenished streams and lakes,
but also on the rocks are its marks engraved
whether we can see them or not. . . .
—JOHN MUIR

Many of the conservation groups that could have been expected to make strong representations at the inquiry were absent or ineffective. Lack of money, staff, information, and coöperation (e.g., with organizations in other jurisdictions) greatly hampered their efforts. Even the Merioneth County Council, though represented by an able advocate, was unable to afford Queen's Counsel to present its—the public's—case. Most of the many hundreds of people and groups that filed written objections were unable to appear in person. The Countryside Commission, formerly the National Parks Commission, stayed out of the whole controversy as long as possible, and finally objected in writing only, though the Commission is the one Government body specifically charged with the protection of the National Parks. The Committee for Environmental Conservation (CoEnCo), a recently formed national coalition of voluntary amenity groups that indirectly represent a total membership of between one and two million people, also was not represented, and filed four paragraphs of written objection only on the insistence of certain of its officials. Finally, the National Farmers' Union, which one might have hoped would oppose industrialization of farmland, supported RTZ because it hoped for fringe benefits such as flood control—another of the topics on which RTZ could not be drawn.

The inquiry revealed three serious flaws in its governing statute, the Town and Country Planning Act, 1962. Firstly, developers are apparently free to divide their schemes into limited, artificially separated stages, each discussed in a separate inquiry to which future stages are deemed to be irrelevant. Thus a road-building authority can propose, one by one, short and individually innocuous sections of road, without mentioning the more controversial governing pattern into which these and later sections are to be linked. Likewise, RTZ could and did insist that test-boring and subsequent hypothetical mining are entirely severable stages of development; RTZ could and did say that until it has done all its test-boring it cannot speculate about the nature of future mining, though the broad outlines of the scheme must by now be plain to everyone; RTZ could and did claim not to know the size and location of possible copper mineralization in Coed-y-brenin, although the company's own geologist had already described in writing the extent of an ore-body delineated by the illegal pre-inquiry drilling; and such evasions and absurdities could not be seriously challenged in the inquiry.

Yet one would have thought the purpose of a planning inquiry was to gather facts on which the Minister could make the decision most in the public interest. To find out the probable consequences of his decision, the Minister must know the developer's plans and consult expert witnesses. It should not be open to an applicant to conceal his plans, to say that because his plans are incomplete they do not exist, or to say that anything beyond the immediate future is too hypothetical to discuss. Of course future events are hypothetical—especially in the sense that they cannot occur if permission for their precursors is denied—but considering the hypothetical is the essence of the inquiry's duty. If planning inquiries are to have anything to do with planning, they must be able to compel an applicant to be candid about his tentative plans—all of them. Until the legal principles by which this can be done are settled, there is no end to the public mischief that developers will cause by exploiting the law's vagueness. They can continue to work on the principle, in effect, that if a burglar comes to your house you have to show him where you keep everything, and if the next night he comes back and walks off with your silver there is no connection whatever with his earlier visit.

Secondly, the 1962 Act requires the determining authority to take into account "the provisions of the development plan, so far as material to the application, and . . . any other material considerations." The decisions in the limited case-law on this provision, rather than construing "material" broadly enough to protect the public interest, seem to leave its construction to the authority concerned. Hence the Secretary of State for Wales will be the judge of whether he has gathered and considered evidence on every "material consideration." The British courts are reluctant to decide what facts are material, since that could require them to become tribunals of fact, so they have not clarified the point of law. (The Inspector at the Dolgellau inquiry was not a lawyer and was not authorized to rule on points of law.) The result of this legal muddle is that planning authorities have an almost free hand in deciding their own terms of reference, and thus in limiting the grounds on which they shall determine applications. Questioning their judgment would probably mean appealing all the way to the House of Lords. I doubt that Parliament meant to give anyone so much executive discretion.

Thirdly, the 1962 Act not only provides that the Secretary's decision cannot be questioned in any court—that his administrative discretion is absolute—but also severely limits the ways in which his decision can be challenged if he has reached it improperly by misdirecting himself on a point of law. The ordinary citizen's prerogative remedies, based on his normal common-law interest in seeing statutes enforced, are largely removed by the Act, and in their place is provided a restricted statutory remedy available only to persons legally injured by the decision. Thus if planning permission for, say, quarrying on land adjacent to yours is granted in a way blatantly contrary to law, you probably have no standing to ask for the decision to be quashed, for you lack a sufficient legal interest. Even those few citizens entitled under the Act to demand its enforcement may have to go to the Lords to succeed—with the risk of having to pay the immense costs of both sides if they lose. I do not understand the need for such a strong deterrent to judicial review. I think it is disgraceful that a planning authority that can already (in practice) make so many of its own rules should also be free to break them without being accountable to any but the most wealthy, persistent, and directly injured landowners. If that is British justice, it badly needs mending.

As I write this in the spring of 1971, the Secretary has received the Inspector's report but has not announced his own decision. Most of the people involved in the running of the Park think that RTZ will probably get most or all of what it has asked for: in effect, sweeping permission to seek evidence that would justify and support a request to allow copper-mining and gold-dredging in Meirion. Many people in England have said to me, "But surely RTZ won't be allowed to mine in the Park!" I hope they are right, but I have no grounds for supposing they will be vindicated by events; RTZ already has at least a foot in the door, and has set its precedent in Yorkshire. And RTZ is only one of many.

I can only hope that the Secretary, in deciding these applications, will recall his speech of 5 October 1970, when the *Liverpool Daily Post* quoted him as saying: "We have come to realise that the quality of life depends more and more on the quality of our environment. Wales is a country of striking natural beauty, although spoiled in places in the past by the relentless advance of industrialisation. Our concern in this European Conservation Year must be two-fold: to preserve and protect from pollution our countryside, towns, rivers and coasts, and to restore where we are able those areas despoiled by man. There is no doubt that the natural environment can no longer be left to take care of itself. Man has an obligation to protect it." I also hope he will apply to RTZ the same reasoning he did to a man to whom he refused permission on 6 October 1969 for a small development involving farm-buildings beside the Mawddach estuary. He wrote then: "The amount of undeveloped coastal and estuarial areas in Britain is relatively small and is diminishing. The point has been reached where every effort should be made to preserve the finest landscape in these areas in its present state." But even if RTZ's present applications are rejected, there will be more, and the fight for Snowdonia will only just be starting. That fight will continue in various forms and places as long as there are minerals in the ground and people who care about National Parks. The tactics will be similar to those I have just described. If the Parks are protected by new laws, miners will work to change or evade the laws. If we want National Parks, we must guard them day by day, and teach our children the same vigilance, for the briefest lapse can lose us what cannot be regained.

While the Secretary's decision is pending, I have found that by a curious feature of English practice, no public stenographer or recordist was present at the Dolgellau inquiry. The only verbatim transcript of the proceedings was taken by a transcripting agency under contract to RTZ. The journalistic records of the inquiry are rather sketchy and include no tape-recording. The only complete précis of arguments presented was the set of minutes taken down by the Inspector, who declines to release it, on the odd ground that it is the basis of his confidential report to the Secretary—a report that by custom, though not by law, will be published when the Secretary announces his decision, and not before. (The Inspector is of course correct; yet the arguments of the inquiry, whatever documents they may be put into, were spoken in public and presumably intended to be heard by the public.) In short, what was supposed to be public knowledge is now private property and is available to an interested member of the public only if one of the parties to the inquiry cares to be put to the trouble of lending a transcript as a courtesy. I think that is a very strange way to run a public inquiry and should be corrected promptly by legislation, for under the present rules an applicant anxious to stifle public debate can simply rely on the complete absence of a record of what he, and everyone else, said at the inquiry. This lack of so simple a remedy as a tape-recorder makes it difficult to prepare a case within the six-week limit allowed for legal action after the Secretary announces his decision; indeed, it may be impossible to question the conduct of an inquiry without having any record of that conduct. If the purpose of a public inquiry is not merely to prevent embarrassment to applicants, but rather to enlist public help in making the decision that will be most in the public interest, the public must have better information, even if they must pay a statutory fee to get it.

I also cannot comprehend—nor could several of the witnesses at the inquiry, though they received no satisfaction on the point—how a company can be entitled to seek legal permission to continue what it has already been doing in knowing violation of the law. I had thought it a well-settled principle of English common law that a party seeking legal help, recognition, or permission must come before the law with clean hands; or, citing a more specialized maxim, from a shameful cause arises no legal action, *ex turpi causa non oritur actio*. The Secretary of State is not a court; yet if I went to my local Inland Revenue Inspector, who is not a court either, and said that I had been evading income-tax for years and wondered if he would mind very much if I went on doing it, I doubt he would be sympathetic. But perhaps the clean-hands principle does not apply to planning law, and perhaps a clever company with a lot of money is in fact entitled to drive a bulldozer through the regulations that Parliament framed to protect all land, including the National Parks, from scandalous abuses.

At the numb root I know winter,
I am marsh. Tattering reeds
Dip broken into ice-logged weeds.
In this cold the beggaring wind
Is an anguish to find rock or tree
That will hold in its stuff
Opposition against me.

—ANTHONY CONRAN
(from "The Marsh")

AMORY LOVINS: Reeds and ice, Llyn Mymbyr Uchaf

6. Economists

IF THE SECRETARY'S decision is substantially in favour of RTZ, it will probably seem in retrospect that a crucial factor was the support RTZ got from the Rural District Councils concerned—against, of course, the sentiments of their County Council. The RDCs, like the local representatives of the national political parties, seem to have been swayed by the economic arguments of RTZ's very able agents: by the exceedingly flimsy proposition that eventual mineral extraction would go a long way to relieve Meirion's chronic economic depression and to improve its standard of living.

I think that what little economic evidence there is wholly fails to support such a view. A prevalent rumour, which RTZ has not publicly denied, says that mining would bring a thousand new jobs to the Park. That is nonsense. An optimistic guess would be several hundred, for a period of from 15 to about 30 years. But to show a profit, RTZ's operations would have to be highly mechanized, and most of the jobs would probably be too skilled to be filled locally. That is one of Professor Allen's grounds for saying that the local employment produced by mining would be relatively small compared to the capital outlay. It is also important to keep in mind that the opening of new mining jobs cannot touch the hard core of local unemployment—the many men disabled by injury and disease in earlier mining and quarrying jobs—and cannot expect to keep young people from emigrating, since a job with no permanence has no attraction. In Llanberis, for example, good jobs on a 15-to-20-year time-scale seem to have almost no attraction for local school-leavers, and may therefore stay unfilled.

How many jobs have recent projects brought to the Park, and how well have the promises of those projects' promoters been fulfilled? The nearest parallel is Anglesey's new RTZ alumina-smelting plant, a huge development for which employment improvements were glowingly forecast. The unemployment rate on Anglesey dropped from 8.1 per cent in and around January 1967 to 7.6 per cent in January 1969, when the construction of the plant was flourishing, but when the building was finished the figure went back up: 8.1 per cent for November 1970. Nor has the earlier Trawsfynydd engineering project in Meirion done as much as had been hoped to reduce unemployment there: many of the labourers were not local Welshmen but imported Irishmen, who have since left the area and taken their money with them, and now that the plant is running, many jobs there are held by Englishmen.

Before suggesting that mining will bring jobs for the local unemployed, RTZ should reflect on the evidence its field geologist gave at the Dolgellau inquiry. He said that the company had had trouble finding locally even six labourers to help the two technicians make the seismic refractory studies of the Mawddach. RTZ should also remember the vulnerability of mineral and metal industries to recession. An RTZ zinc plant in South Wales, for example, has just been forced to close (with the loss of 680 jobs) because, as *The Times* quoted the Executive Director, "The industry has been overbuilt. We just can't sell all we make." Is there any guarantee that such miscalculations will not recur?

The strategic and foreign-exchange arguments for RTZ's schemes are in broad outline unconvincing. It is true that Britain spends a hundred million pounds a year on importing copper, and that the biggest present sources are unstable—Chile because of mine nationalization and Zambia because of Britain's supplying arms to South Africa (a policy that is so controversial in the rest of Africa as to be potentially disastrous to all Britain's interests there). Yet firstly, there are many relatively stable sources of copper—RTZ, for example, has huge mines in South Africa, New Guinea, and British Columbia. Secondly, to the extent that RTZ's capital comes from abroad, its profits would be liable to return thither, reducing the saving in sterling. Thirdly, neither domestic copper nor the sterling it might save would appear magically out of the air: they would come out of the ground, depleting in a rather short time an irreplaceable resource which, the strategists tell us, could be essential in a national emergency later. Fourthly, in return for a short-term gain Britain would have to accept a permanent loss, not only in minerals but also, more importantly, in the beauty and the civilized values that make Britain a desirable place to live in—the qualities, for example, that re-create visitors to Britain's wild places—and in the stable long-term benefits, direct and indirect, that these qualities would normally produce.

Working mines and dredgers are often represented as tourist attractions, but I know of no evidence that such projects elsewhere in Britain act as anything but a deterrent to tourism. Tourists will not come to look at a dead landscape, and I doubt they could be persuaded to come watch it being killed. Mining would substitute highly speculative, short-term, undispersed income, whose very existence there is reason to question, for the known, substantial, and permanent income available from tourism—income that now, though only partly exploited, brings more than £5 million ($12 million) a year to Merioneth (about £400 a year for each family), and whose benefit reaches nearly everyone in the community. In other words, a short-sighted exploitative policy would in the long run do far more harm than good to the Park's economy, for it would destroy the Park's most permanent values: it would bring to the Dolgellau area the same chronic depression and everlasting devastation that the slate-quarries have brought to Llanberis. Those who favour mining in the Park must ask themselves if they want their children to live with the waste-heaps. Can they have forgotten so quickly that in their fathers' time, men slaved in the quarries so that their children could go anywhere but in the quarries?

Our technology cannot do everything. We must not deceive ourselves into thinking that estuarine dredging and opencast mining are reversible processes. If we knew how to restore land thus despoiled to a semblance of its original state—which we do not—we would find the cost greater than the original investment. Even under ideal conditions, with no mining wastes to contend with, we have neither the money nor the ability to make even a simple and small sort of beautiful place, let alone a Mawddach or a Coed-y-brenin. We would be wiser to leave such tasks to the forces accustomed to doing them, lest the Mawddach, which has been famous for centuries for its beauty, become infamous for many more centuries for its hideousness. To reserve a proportion of RTZ's profits for "cosmeticizing" the lunar landscape created by its activities, as some people have suggested, would be like robbing and murdering a man—and piously devoting part of the proceeds to helping his widow buy a pretty tombstone.

"Those who will not remember history," said Santayana, "are condemned to relive it." Always with me are the ghosts of Hetch Hetchy, Glen Canyon, and the other beautiful places that we have lost to the exploiters because, in our apathy, we thought it did not matter, or that if it did matter, there were many other places like them. We now know that it does matter, and that there are no other places. There is no spare earth. We must make the best of the one earth we have, and try to use it in a way that our children will call wise.

It is no wisdom to measure all good by the Gross National Product. We can inflate the GNP by employing one man to dump industrial wastes into a river and another man to filter them out again; but is that what we want? An official of the National Farmers' Union recently lamented that in the Mawddach, "where once you had . . . waving corn and the hum of threshing machines, you now have bullrush and wild duck." No doubt corn is useful and would profit the farmer more, but then why not plant corn all over Hyde Park? Is wealth the same as happiness?

It is customary to say that we must devise ways of costing wildness and beauty so that we can include the explicit value of their loss in our cost-benefit calculations (not the value of their gain, for we cannot create them). I am not going to say that. I think it is silly. Economics is undoubtedly an important and valuable science, but it has limits. It will never help me decide which of the late quartets of Beethoven is best, or even whether cornfields are better than wildfowl-marshes. Making decisions is always painful, but I cannot escape the responsibility for my decisions by attributing them to oracular numbers, and it would be dishonest to try to. Men of good will made complex decisions before cost-benefit analysis was invented, and I believe they still can. Human conscience still

We do not feel proud enough of being alive.

—Geoffrey Winthrop Young

exists. There is no substitute for it. Adopting the methods of our machines will only make us machinelike; and if we have trouble fitting some types of permanent values into our calculations, the rational remedy is not to change the values but to change our methods, in order to make it harder to hide our meaning from ourselves. Turning words into numbers when it is inappropriate to do so gives us no information or insights that we lacked before, but only slides a new and more opaque layer of abstraction between our perceptions and the world they reflect. Therefore I shall not propose that the spiritual values of the Park be quantified, but only that they be perceived, so that they can speak for themselves—not as arbitrary numbers but as living experience.

It is up to this generation to decide whether the old ways of making a living from the land are necessarily the best ways, or whether the cost is so great for those who come after that better ways should be sought. In the Snowdonia National Park, we have inherited one of the most beautiful wild places in the world. Before we pass it on to our children as a desert, we should ask whether the benefit will be worth the cost—not the benefit to a few mining consortia but the benefit to us, and not the cost to us alone but the cost to every generation after us, to whom we are stewards answerable for what we lose. I hope the people of Britain will agree with me that, to paraphrase Newton Drury, Britain is neither rich enough to be able to afford to sell Snowdonia, nor poor enough to need to.

AMORY LOVINS: Clogwyn-y-garnedd

We have abolished superstition of the heart
only to install a superstition of the intellect in its place.
We behave as if there were some magic in mere thought,
and we use thinking for purposes for which it was never designed.
As a result we are no longer sufficiently aware
of the importance of what we cannot know intellectually,
what we must know in other ways, of the living experience
before and beyond our transistory knowledge.

—LAURENS VAN DER POST

PHILIP EVANS: Detail near Llyn Bwlch Cwm-llan

He who knows nothing, loves nothing.
He who can do nothing understands nothing.
He who understands nothing is worthless.
But he who understands also loves, notices, sees. . . .
The more knowledge is inherent in a thing, the greater the love.

—PARACELSUS
(*quoted by* ERICH FROMM)

7. Administrators

THERE IS SAID to be a maxim in Washington: "If you can't solve a problem any other way, throw money at it." In the Snowdonia National Park, this technique would not work. Of course the Park needs money, both for urgent remedial projects and for longer-term injection into new ventures; but if money were miraculously to appear tomorrow, it could not be properly used, for the Park's defects of function would stall planning and action. I think that most of these defects of function are due to defects of structure, and to wrong assumptions about how a Park should be run.

Underlying the problem of administering the Park is an uneasy compromise, fixed by the National Parks Act of 1949, between private ownership and public use of the land. In the best tradition of British compromise, this one worked fairly well—until the public use became too heavy. But even though the compromise has now largely broken down, we must continue to live with it, for the concept of private ownership is probably too firmly entrenched to permit any sudden change from private to State ownership. That is not to say that the State cannot buy any tracts of Park land that come onto the market. The State did just this in April 1968 with the 13,000-acre Vaynol tract (including the central and northwest part of the Snowdon massif, most of Llanberis Pass, the southwest side of the Glyder, and several peaks between Nantlle and Rhyd-ddu), and if the State can ever make up its mind what to do with the land now that it has got it, the results may encourage other such purchases.

Yet the compromise inherent in the National Parks Act is a form of trying to have your cake and eat it too: trying to carry on unchanged the normal life of the countryside while at the same time admitting for dozens of kinds of outdoor recreation a flood of foreign visitors who may think the land belongs to them. All this can be done, but not without some adjustments somewhere. It would be natural to expect that land designated as a National Park would, as a concession to its changed use, be administered differently; but this is the case only in theory, not in reality. The National Parks Act has very few special effects on administration, and the only significant difference between Park and non-Park land in any particular County is that the planning controls exercised by the local authority are in practice slightly stricter in the former. Aside from this difference (for which there is probably no direct legal requirement), no significant protection accrues to the Park under the provisions of the Act. Parliament has never even said that the aims of National Parks (quoted at the start of section four, above) preclude the pursuit in those Parks of practices, such as large-scale mining, that are clearly inconsistent with those aims. Hence almost every Park in Britain contains some large intrusion that ought

not to be there. Dartmoor National Park is still the site of massive military exercises; several Parks contain big quarries and mines; the Pembrokeshire Coast National Park is hedged in by vast oil-refineries; the Parks overflow with examples of disastrous compromise between principle and profit.

Before the 1949 Act was passed, planning legislation had zoned the country according to the acceptability of extensive development, and practically the whole Snowdonia National Park (as it was later declared) was then classified as a "white area," one that was intended to remain roughly as it was and in which there was a strong presumption against substantial development. It is hard to see what specific protection the 1949 Act adds to this classification. If large-scale mining is allowed in the Park, it will indeed seem, in Jon Tinker's words, that "declaring a national park does little more than entitle the area to a 75 per cent Treasury grant for public lavatories."

The adaptation of the Park's administrative structure from pre-Park forms has been mostly on paper. When the Park was first designated in 1951, the three constituent County Councils discussed for 16 months whether to administer it with a Joint Board—the normal procedure intended by Parliament for multi-County Parks—or with separate local boards advised by a Joint Advisory Committee (JAC). The County Councils refused to have the Joint Board, and for reasons that were not convincing at the time and are certainly invalid now, the Minister, under intense County pressure, finally overruled the National Parks Commission and agreed to the troika-and-JAC scheme, at first on a trial basis and then permanently. The result is the well-intentioned but ineffectual machinery that runs the Park today.

Each of the constituent County Councils is required by the 1949 Act to delegate all planning functions for the parts of its County that lie within the Park to a special subcommittee, two-thirds of whose members are appointed by the Council directly and the remaining third by the Council on the nomination of the Secretary of State for Wales. It is these three Park Planning Committees that actually control the future of the Park, but they are three, not one, and their interests often diverge. They are under no effective outside control except, sometimes, that of the Secretary.

The three Park Planning Committees must refer certain sorts of proposals—in effect, all important plans for development—to the JAC and its Planning Consultant for advice. The JAC is the only official body that has extensive local knowledge and that represents all the major interests in the Park; it consists of 16 councillors and aldermen (eight from Merioneth, six from Caernarvonshire, two from Denbighshire) plus eight other people appointed by the local Councils jointly on nomination by the Secretary of State for Wales advised by the National Parks Commission (now the Countryside Commission). If you think that the local Councils should be advised by a supposedly independent body that they can in fact completely control, this will sound to you like a good scheme. (The Commission that drafted the 1949 legislation wanted each Park Committee to have its Chairman and half its members appointed by the National Parks Commission, the other half by the County Councils, and the Planning Officer by both.) The trouble is that the JAC is by law a purely advisory body with no executive powers; the County and District Councils are free to ignore its advice and to decide major issues on purely local economic and political grounds.

This distribution of power is unsatisfactory. The Park administration as now set up cannot do its job effectively, and I do not see how it ever can. With the best will in the world, three local bodies made up predominantly of local Council members (who are supposed to uphold the interests of their constituents) cannot be expected to agree on important Park-wide issues, far less to represent the interests of the whole Park. Nor can the very considerable talent and dedication now scattered through the many fragmented Park authorities be brought to bear on the Park's most urgent problems.

The diffusion of the Park's administration has three harmful effects. The first of these we have just mentioned: that decisions cannot be made for the whole Park, nor can the people who are concerned with the whole Park make decisions that have force. The second is that as long as the Park is run by a troika, it must continue to drift without a general plan. The urgent need for Park-wide planning on traffic management, campsites and tourist amenities, waterway use, footpath maintenance, and other perennial problems cannot be met by an administrative structure so diffused that it seems to be a mechanism for avoiding decision-making. The Park, in short, is free to deteriorate because its complex problems are being treated piecemeal as they arise in each of the three Counties.

Finally, responsibility for matters affecting large areas of the Park is distributed through so many small, overworked, and poorly funded departments that a single local official who conceives his duties narrowly or does not work well with his colleagues can bring to a halt the whole mechanism of the Park in his County. For example, Acts passed in 1949 and 1968 called for Definitive Footpath Maps (showing exactly where walkers may and may not go) to be issued as soon as possible. The Merioneth authorities issued theirs in 1964 and updated it in 1969. Yet in Caernarvonshire, where there is at least as much money available, the map has been hanging fire for over 20 years because the local officials cannot coördinate their activities. The amount of work to be done is not excessive—only a few of the 21 disputed rights-of-way may have to be resolved in court—but there is no date even for issuing a provisional edition. Much of the ill-feeling between farmers and hikers in Eryri is due directly to this failure.

A typical Park-wide problem now being dealt with disjointedly is the use of waterways, most of which are owned or leased by anglers. Conflicts of interest with canoeists, power-boaters, water-skiers, sailors, and swimmers are bound to arise more and more, and the fishing-rights now held by a few men who pay heavily for them are increasingly coveted by the less affluent majority of anglers. In one or two specific cases (e.g., Llyn Geirionnydd in 1968), a Council has decreed zoning to end the confusion, and there are signs that the Caernarvonshire authorities hope eventually to deter power-boating. Yet the three Councils have not managed to agree with themselves, let alone with each other, on the broad questions of waterway use, even though the issues will obviously have to be settled everywhere sooner or later, and it is both inefficient and futile to settle them only locally or *ad hoc*.

The natural administrative division of Britain is highland-*vs*-lowland and urban-*vs*-rural. For two decades there has been talk of combining the county governments into larger regional units whose boundaries would be determined by natural divisions rather than by the accidents of history. So far this talk has come to nothing, though the new Conservative Government has just announced (February 1971) that it hopes to effect these reforms in three years. But as might be expected, the local governments oppose reorganization as a plot by their neighbours. Anglesey and Merioneth, for example, would both object to being swallowed by Caernarvonshire, which has a greater population than both of them together; yet this consolidation would come close to reconstituting the obviously healthy ancient region of Gwynedd (Arfon and Arllechwedd) plus Môn. This area has been largely a single economic, social, and geographic unit since time immemorial, and still is.

Whether or not the County governments are consolidated, that of the Park must be. There must be a Unitary Authority for the Park (as the Redcliffe-Maud report suggested for all the Parks), able to calculate priorities and make comprehensive plans—and empowered to put them into practice. It may be argued that such centralization of power is contrary to British tradition. But the people of the Park are now dictated to by London and Cardiff, and I should have thought it better to be dictated to by their own people, who have at heart the interests of the unified Park and who know its values and problems at firsthand. The present scheme fails to confer the potential benefit of local control, namely freedom from outside exploitation (quite the opposite), but has all the drawbacks of isolated and dilatory local government.

It may also be argued that if the Park became a Unitary Authority, the jurisdiction of the Caernarvonshire authorities would dwindle to a small, densely populated strip along the north coast. That is true, and would infuriate the County Council, but it cannot be helped. Caernarvonshire's present fusion of northern towns with southern farms is an administrative monstrosity and serves the interests of neither area. The easiest solution would be to fuse the governments of the Counties (readjusting the boundary if necessary on the Denbighshire side) so that there would be no Caernarvonshire authorities as such to feel deprived. Failing that, perhaps they, and their similarly deprived neighbours in Merioneth, might be mollified if part of the rates from their former areas continued to be paid into County funds during a long transitional period.

A Unitary Authority for the Park would have to be set up very carefully, and the constituent authorities would have to be convinced that they would be better off if they sacrificed some sovereignty in order to work together. In mid-Wales, a rural development board covering a large area has already run into trouble because its enabling legislation, although designed to aid farmers, contained a compulsory-purchase-of-farms provision that turned the residents against the whole idea. Likewise, a recent proposal for setting up a National Park in the wild and beautiful Cambrian Mountains along the spine of mid-Wales has been locally condemned as a

paternalistic land-grab. Mistakes like these must be avoided. But there are highly successful precedents for unified Parks. Northern England's Peak District National Park overlaps even more jurisdictions than Snowdonia does—it includes parts of four Counties and a City, even though it is mostly in one County (Derbyshire) and is only two-thirds the size of Snowdonia. Of course there is no precedent exactly in point, but as Lord Mildew remarked, "There is no precedent for anything until it is done for the first time." I think the Snowdonia National Park is worth a bit of innovation. It will take quite a lot, though, for the Conservative Government has just issued a White Paper abandoning the Redcliffe-Maud proposal for Unitary Authorities in the ten National Parks that together cover 9 per cent of the area of England and Wales. The White Paper proposes instead that the administration be left in the hands of the same County Council committees that have shown themselves, in eight of the ten Parks, consistently incapable of acting in the Parks' long-term interests. This decision must be overturned if the Parks are ever to be administered properly. The basic flaw lies in the system of Park Planning Committees, and the amalgamation of the three

PHILIP EVANS: The Cantilever, Glyder Fach

. . . a region where the upright lava-ledges had been slit asunder into chasms, crushed together into caves,
toppled over each other, hurled up into spires, in such chaotic confusion that progress seemed impossible.

—CHARLES KINGSLEY

Committees into one for all Gwynedd would not be an adequate reform.

In theory, giving the Snowdonia National Park a single effective administrative machine would not need drastic new legislation, for much of the groundwork has been laid in the Countryside Act, 1968. Unfortunately, Parliament has not seen fit to fund the Countryside Commission (created by the Act out of the National Parks Commission) at the £2-million ($4.8-million) annual level originally contemplated. This year's appropriation is about £516,000 for the Commission itself plus £205,000 for grants to the National Parks. This total of £721,000 compares with an annual Exchequer authorization of £16 million for the Forestry Commission, £1.4 million for Royal Parks and Pleasure Gardens, £38 million for atomic energy, £332 million for highway-building, £188 million for nonmilitary aerospace work, and £2280 million for defence. Last year, the Countryside Commission got from the Government only 30 pence per £100 of what that Government has spent so far on the Concorde aircraft.

The Countryside Commission now has a staff of about 90, two-thirds the number planned for 1968. It therefore cannot fulfil its functions, which "are to be exercised for the conservation and enhancement of the natural beauty and amenity of the countryside, and encouraging the provision and improvement, for persons resorting to the countryside, of facilities for the enjoyment of the countryside, and of open-air recreation in the countryside." The 1968 Act contains sweeping provisions for ordering changes in the Park, financing amenities and tourist developments, regulating traffic, appointing wardens, and planning Park policy; but without money these provisions are all useless. Britain's renamed National Parks Commission cannot afford to discharge its duties to the nation, and nobody else can discharge them instead.

Parliament's reluctance to appropriate appropriately leaves the impression that it wants something for nothing or at least is sublimating intention into wish. There is a tendency in all legislatures, and especially in those that have refined the elegant use of language, to think there is some magic in words —"to dance," as a physicist friend recently put it, "upon a corkscrew of words, and to think that what the words say is thereby carried out." But repeating the word "countryside" four times in a sentence does not mend a single path, pay a single warden, or stop a single exploiter.

The remedy is as near as your desk. To paraphrase a recent issue of *Not Man Apart* (the Friends of the Earth newsletter): "Parliament does one of two things: what you want it to do, or what it thinks you don't care if it does. Have you written your MP a do-and-don't letter? Why not? Your elected representatives can't help stomping on your toes if they don't know where your toes are. If, knowing, they still stomp, stomp back at election time. You always know where *their* toes are."

PHILIP EVANS: Feral goats near Heather Terrace, Tryfan

Let us suppose, then, that you have made Parliament realize the limited effect of speechmaking, and that the Park has been given a unified administration with the executive powers it needs, derived either from special legislation or from the Countryside Commission and Act. What ought the Park authorities to do next? The answer, I think, would make a very long book, and I am not the man to write it; the JAC, the Nature Conservancy, and other bodies long active in the Park contain experts much better fitted than I to plot the course of the Park. I have only tried here to set out some of the options, and to tell you enough of the facts to help you judge, as all citizens must do, whether future proposals are likely to aid or harm the Park. But several suggestions have already appeared in the previous pages of this book, and you may like to see some of the more important ones collected here in one place.

But our civilization is rapidly becoming one in which
only two values are recognized: power and amusement. . . .
Gradually one has heard less and less about "preserving," more
and more about "development" and "utilization for recreation."
The two ideals are neither identical nor even compatible.
—JOSEPH WOOD KRUTCH

First, the purposes of the Park, as set out by Parliament, can be furthered by certain land-uses and impeded by others. A comprehensive land- (and water-) use plan for the whole Park is an urgent priority. It should be possible to decide on principle, once and for all, whether large-scale mineral extraction is compatible with the intended functions of a National Park. At least the power to authorize prospecting and mining in National Parks should be reserved to Parliament, on the principle that a Park set up by Parliament should not be subject to destruction except by Parliament, acting in free and open debate before the public.

Second, ways must be sought and implemented to make the Park self-supporting, but this must not be planned by economists imported from elsewhere unless they are willing to give full weight to the preservation of the rural culture. Both year-round quasi-cottage industry and seasonal tourist industry must be village-based. Some forms that both sorts of development might take have already been set out above. Tourist development should be coördinated with education through the Wales Tourist Board, the national school system, and local information centres (such as the one in the Lake District that had more than 100,000 visitors in its first full season). The JAC's recent pamphlet on the Park is an excellent start at giving visitors a better understanding of how the countryside works.

Third, the urgent needs of the visitors to the Park must be met as described earlier—needs ranging from campsites to footpaths to maps. It is essential that these amenities be built under centralized direction and under a Park-wide plan, not allowed to grow haphazardly as in the past, and that the Park's long-range recreation plan be based upon a clear idea of what the Park's functions are to be and what sorts of activities it wants to attract. More tourists should be diverted into the forests and the less-frequented ranges, especially in Meirion, in order to distribute the wear, although the wildest areas should be left to attract only the highly motivated solitude-seeker as they do now. Essential services, including mountain rescue, must be properly funded and coördinated. The Park Authority must be empowered to encourage and advise farmers who wish to set up acceptably landscaped tourist enterprises, and should prepare an easy-to-read pamphlet (analogous to that of the U.S. Department of Agriculture) on the financial, legal, and practical aspects of doing so. Private investment in tourist developments peripheral to the Park should also be stimulated, if necessary by offering as a bait the franchise options for further specified expansion.

Fourth, the Park must have, quickly, a road and traffic plan coördinated with adjacent authorities. In the long run, through traffic should be rerouted around the Park and extensive automobile traffic within the Park should be strongly discouraged, for if motor traffic continues to gobble up the Park at the present rate, there will soon be little room for

people. Traffic planning should consider that in a few decades the private car will be a rare luxury. Wherever possible, cars should be left at the edge of the Park, and further transport limited to Park minibuses, as is done very successfully in other Parks throughout the world (including part of the English Peak District). Planning and enforcing a decline in auto traffic will take vision and firmness, but I think Snowdonia is worth it. Otherwise cars and new roads will do to Eryri what they have done to the Lake District. And not only must the Park be kept from becoming a bit of greenery around the trunk roads, but coming to the Park, and especially to its wilder sections, must not be made too convenient: it is possible to sort out many of the potential visitors who would be unsympathetic to the land simply by so designing access to and within the Park that only those people who seriously want to go there, rather than to more urbanized country parks, will undertake the journey.

Fifth, both to protect the land and to advise and assist the public, the Park should have an adequate professional warden service, using a combination of full-time staff wardens and part-time volunteers. I think good people would be easy to find, both in the eager mountain-lovers of the north coast and in the residents of the Park itself. (Native wardens are always best if you can get them. I can think of no better full-time warden than a middle-aged farmer, or his son, who wants to reduce his stock but still make a living on the land, for he loves the land, knows it intimately, and communicates well. Many farmers could be said now to be involuntary wardens distracted by sheep-farming. It would make every sort of sense to pay a decent wage to those who want to be wardens officially.) The functions of wardens, as set out in the 1949 and 1968 Acts, are very broad, but consist mainly of public relations (among visitors, residents, and the lecture-going public), directing volunteer projects, and guiding walks. The present burden of routine maintenance—wall- and path-rebuilding, litter-collecting, and the like—should be transferred to a mobile (but unmechanized) unit set up for the purpose. The Park's present amenity groups and the Nature Conservancy should be brought wherever possible into the information and warden projects of the Park; for example, the much-needed information-centre in Llanberis, a potential wet-weather haven, would be a fine place for exhibits and slideshows on natural history. The Conservancy should also be asked to help train professional wardens, and paid to expand its present services for visitors to its Nature Reserves. These are not new proposals; they are an attempt to collect some of the best practices now followed in other British National Parks—with whose wardens, as with those from Parks throughout the world, there should be far more comparing of notes.

Sixth, the Park Authority, through the Secretary of State for Wales, should use the important Vaynol purchase as a testing-ground for new policies of integrated land-use, including the controlled development of tourist enterprises as a part of hill-farming. When the Government bought this land in 1968, the announced motive, "to secure public enjoyment of this area of great natural beauty," was coupled with a promise that "provision for public access and other facilities would be made" along with "determination of the properties to be offered for sale to tenants." I have seen no evidence that any of these aims have been realized. The Government seems not to have bought the mineral rights (which are now reportedly vested in a firm of mineral agents), and will probably dodge its public responsibility by selling most of the land back to the tenants, who could then do with it anything for which they (or a mining company) could get planning permission. This is not a propitious start. The promised use of the Vaynol land for recreation should be effected promptly, and the whole tract used as a laboratory for the Park Authority's ideas about Park management—about how to reconcile the interests of farmers and visitors. The Government should also take advantage of its chance to provide proper campsites at Nant Peris, Pen-y-pàs, and Rhyd-ddu, and thus prevent haphazard camping nearby, e.g., in Llanberis Pass.

I must not be understood to say that the Park should be overrun by officious busybodies wearing wardens' badges; nor spattered with hot-dog stands and souvenir shops as "tourist developments"; nor, on the other hand, sealed against all intrusions, whether by people from the cities or by money for the residents, as though the life of the Park could be arrested in mid-heartbeat or returned to the simpler forms of decades ago. If you have followed this far the story of the Park, I think you will agree with me that all these courses are abhorrent, and in the interest of neither the Park nor the nation. I hope you will also share my faith that light industry, in the form of one-storey factories built among the houses of the villages, could be assimilated into the visual and cultural fabric of the Park; that there is a right way to encourage tourism; and that if the people now concerned with the Park are given a proper chance to run it under a sensible régime, they will be able to use cottage industry and tourism as constructive forces to preserve the best values of the Park's culture and scenery.

If these things are done, Snowdonia could become the first National Park in Britain to meet the minimum standards of protection required for inclusion in the United Nations List of National Parks and Equivalent Reserves.

JOHN CLEARE: Yr Elen

8. Citizens

What doth he here, Man that is born of woman?
The clouds may haunt these mountains; the fierce storm
Coiled in his caverned lair—that wild torrent
Leaps from a native land: but Man! O Lord!
What doth he here!

—ROBERT STEPHEN HAWKER (1832)

I SUGGESTED much earlier that if the decline of hill-farming continued, the lack of grazing would let the moors revert to impenetrable thicket and then to forest. We do not know all the details, despite the Nature Conservancy's pioneering studies of land-regeneration, but it seems likely that a birch or alder phase could even lead to a resurgence of oak forest. I hope that a long-range plan for the Park will consider whether it might be desirable to let an uninhabited part of the Park revert in this way. It really depends on whether this is the way Britain wants her Park to be. I do not propose such a laissez-faire policy for very much of the Park, however, because I respect the venerable culture that depends on pastoralism, and I do not know how adaptable that culture would be to changes of habitat.

This argument raises the broader question of whether rural depopulation is bad. Human communities, like any other communities, follow ecological principles, and artificially maintaining a community in an inappropriate habitat takes a lot of energy and strains the whole ecosystem. Hence I do not see any strong ground for maintaining the population of, say, Sutherland (where the residents have altered the landscape less drastically than in Eryri)—so long as people who want to live in Sutherland will always be able to do so, on the land's own terms. The reason I feel different about Eryri is that its residents (whose economy has become precarious only through external forces, not through any inherent unsuitability of the habitat) do want to continue to live there and to maintain their unique indigenous culture. I think they should have the opportunity. It is a peculiar arrogance of civilized cultures, especially in our modern cities, to think that everyone ought to be happy in the same (urban) niche. This is not true of any other species, and I do not think it is true of ours. Eryri and Meirion are part of our essential human and scenic diversity.

It is this diversity, the greatest wealth of our planet, that gives the Park much of its atmosphere of wildness, for diversity is the very element our cities lack. David Brower was not thinking of a man-made monoculture such as Los Angeles when he wrote of ". . . a place where you can be serene, that will let you contemplate and connect two consecutive thoughts, or that if need be can stir you up as you were made to be stirred up, until you blend with the wind and water and earth you almost forgot you came from." The diversity of wildness cannot be artificially created: it flows from the evolutionary force we are busily repudiating. What diversity we have now is a legacy we cannot increase and are under no order to diminish. Our talents seem to run to making deserts, not to making wildness.

Aros a Myned

Aros mae'r mynyddau mawr,
　Rhuo trostynt mae y gwynt;
Clywir eto gyda'r wawr
　Gân bugeiliaid megis cynt.
Eto tyf y llygad dydd
　O gylch traed y graig a'r bryn,
Ond bugeiliaid newydd sydd
　Ar yr hen fynyddoedd hyn.

Ar arferion Cymru gynt
　Newid ddaeth o rod i rod;
Mae cenhedlaeth wedi mynd
　A chenhedlaeth wedi dod.
Wedi oes dymhestlog hir
　Alun Mabon mwy nid yw,
Ond mae'r heniaith yn y tir
　A'r alawon hen yn fyw.

　　　　　　　—Ceiriog (1832-87)

Yet though we cannot make a wild place, we can inherit one and for a time be stewards of it. In this way we have come to have the wild place we call the Snowdonia National Park: living land and living people. Will the life remain?

That depends on how you feel about your National Park. Perhaps you think that it is good to have, somewhere in Britain, a few people who don't drive a car in a loop between the factory and the television set—people who still know how to sing, how to pick a good ram, and what the clouds mean. If you like this idea, do you say so? Perhaps you like the thought of having some real mountains left so that your children, if they choose to, can see them face to face, not as we see the dodo in the museum. If you agree, do you say so? Perhaps you are willing to pay a few pennies more for your water or electricity, or drive a few minutes more to get from here to there, or let some shares in the Stock Exchange stay a few points lower, in order to give your grandchildren the wild valleys your parents gave you. Do you say so? Do you feel obliged to say so?

None of these wishes will come true unless you want them enough. You have to be heard. David Brower, when someone asked "What can *I* say?" replied: "We have no blueprint. We offer no substitute here for citizenship and its requirement that each citizen who is concerned about his society and his world should contribute a tithe of his own sweat. We offer no easy way to sweat. The only way out is *through* and you have to involve yourself. Either that or plead guilty when your children ask what happened to the beautiful world you inherited." If you want to be able, with honesty, to tell your children something else, there is no time but the present; and if enough of your fellow-citizens join you in making known their longing that their children may have wild places left to come home to, then that longing will be fulfilled, and our children will inherit the earth: a whole earth.

Epilogue

A light was upon it for which his language had no name.
All that he saw was shapely, but the shapes seemed at once clear cut,
as if they had been first conceived and drawn at the uncovering of his eyes,
and ancient as if they had endured for ever.
He saw no colour but those he knew, gold and white
and blue and green, but they were fresh and poignant,
as if he had at that moment first perceived them
and made for them names new and wonderful.

—J. R. R. TOLKIEN

. . . Gwawl a gwres haul a glaw grisialaidd,
Rhamant y rhod a miragl tyn horau,
Yn gweithio'n ir yn eu gwythi aneirif . . .

—THOMAS GWYNN JONES (1871-1949)

. . . Sunlight, and warmth, and the crystal rain,
World-wonder, the wheel, the miracle of seasons,
Labouring green through innumerable veins . . .

—(translated by ANTHONY CONRAN)

We forget that nature itself is one vast miracle
transcending the reality of night and nothingness.
We forget that each one of us in his personal life
repeats that miracle.

—LOREN EISELEY

ELIZABETH A. R. PHIPPS: Glaslyn

. . . majesty, and beauty, and repose,
A blended holiness of earth and sky,
Something that makes this individual spot,
This small abiding-place of many men,
A termination, and a last retreat,
A centre, come from wheresoe'er you will,
A whole without dependence or defect,
Made for itself, and happy in itself,
Perfect contentment, unity entire. . . .

—WORDSWORTH (1800)

PHILIP EVANS: Northern Carneddau

What is the use of a house if you haven't got a tolerable planet to put it on?

—THOREAU

PHILIP EVANS: Cader Idris

The Secret Springs

Where are the secret springs, and where
The hidden source of sudden joy?
Whence is the laughter, like the torrent, falling? Whence
The tears, the rainbow-scattered sunlight, overhead?

Over the pinewood and the pasture and the pathway
Rises the rockface where the bootnails scratch
Smooth mossy walls, and the blind fingers reach
Damp ferns in crevices, and icy pools.

Water on brant and slape; the little streams
Rise in the gullies and the squelching moss:
Somewhere above the chockstone springs
Joy, and the sudden halt of tiny grief.

Summer will dry the rock-pool; winter bind
These, and the immortelles will bloom
In memory, and in memory only, these
Slow drops will fall.

Somewhere above the rockrose and the lichen,
Even in summer, or midwinter, moves
The powder-snow, the changing counterpart
Of changing, and unchanging, sea.

Somewhere above the step, the springs of action
Rise, and the snow falls, and the séracs; and the green glacier-ice
Moves down like history, or like the huge
Slow movement of a nation's mind.

Somewhere above the ice, unwitnessed storms
Break in the darkness on the summit ridge
And the white whirling avalanche
Blends with the storm, the night, the driven snow;

And sunlight, and the dark, and gravitation,
These are all: these are the hidden springs, simplicity,
And darkness is
The epitome of light, and darkness, and all lonely places.

—MICHAEL ROBERTS

I take infinite pains to know all the phenomena of spring, . . .
thinking that I have here the entire poem, and then, to my chagrin,
I learn that it is but an imperfect copy that I possess and have read,
that my ancestors have torn out many of the first leaves
and grandest passages, and mutilated it in many places.
I should not like to think that some demigod had come before me
and picked out some of the best of the stars.
I wish to know an entire heaven and an entire earth.

*—*THOREAU

Mae'r oll yn gysegredig, mae barddoniaeth
Nefolaidd ar yr holl fynyddoedd hyn. . . .

—Islwyn (1832-78)

Everything is sacred, all these mountains
Have in them heavenly music. . . .

—translated by Anthony Conran
(from "The Storm")

The River

And the cobbled water
Of the stream with the trout's indelible
Shadows that winter
Has not erased—I walk it
Again under a clean
Sky with the fish, speckled like thrushes,
Silently singing among the weed's
Branches.

    I bring the heart
Not the mind to the interpretation
Of their music, letting the stream
Comb me, feeling it fresh
In my veins, revisiting the sources
That are as near now
As on the morning I set out from them.

        —R. S. Thomas

We travel together, passengers on a little space ship,
dependent upon its vulnerable reserves of air and soil,
committed for our safety to its security and peace,
preserved from annihilation only by the care, the work
and, I will say, the love we give our fragile craft.
We cannot maintain it half-fortunate, half-miserable,
half-confident, half-despairing, half-free
in a liberation of resources undreamed of until this day,
half-slave to the ancient enemies of man.
No craft, no crew, can travel safely with such vast contradictions.
On their resolution depends the survival of us all.

—ADLAI STEVENSON
Geneva, July 1965

The Earth's Wild Places: 5

A FRIENDS OF THE EARTH SERIES
in collaboration with the John Muir Institute of Environmental Studies

The John Muir Institute and Friends of the Earth serve a common purpose: the preservation, restoration, and rational use of the earth. The Muir Institute, founded in New Mexico in 1968, is tax-deductible. It assumes that the conservation cause deserves an improved flow of better information, and seeks to accomplish this through scientific, educational, and literary means. Friends of the Earth, founded in New York in 1969, assumes that unless there is action now based upon what information we already have, then our researchers may never complete their studies. Friends of the Earth believes it can act adequately only if it is not tax-deductible, and it isn't.

Working in tandem, complementing each other, properly separating funds and combining their effort, Muir and Friends seek to help existing conservation organizations get new things accomplished. Together they try to persuade people here and abroad that survival is scientifically and politically feasible.

The John Muir Institute is responsible for assembling the illustrated, edited manuscripts for the international exhibit series, The Earth's Wild Places, to portray the beauty, diversity, and organic wholeness of life and the natural environment of the planet. Friends of the Earth thereupon publishes under contract with The McCall Publishing Company. The series is under the general editorship of David R. Brower, who initiated the exhibit format series when serving as executive director of the Sierra Club and was general editor for the club of the first twenty volumes of the series.

Joint Offices: San Francisco, New York, Washington, Anchorage, Albuquerque, Seattle, Honolulu, Paris, London, Zurich, Stockholm.

Principal Addresses: 451 Pacific Avenue, San Francisco 94133; 30 East 42nd Street, New York, New York 10017; 917 15th Street, N.W., Washington, D.C. 20005; Box 1977, Anchorage, Alaska 99501; 8016 Zuni Road, S.E., Albuquerque, New Mexico 87108; Les Amis de la Terre, 25 Quai Voltaire, Paris; Friends of the Earth, Ltd., 8 King Street, London W.C. 2, England; Im Bruggen, 8903 Bonstetten (Zh); Jordens Vänner, Linnegatan 3, Stockholm.

Ecosphere Associates (editorial board for The Earth's Wild Places): David R. Brower, Donald W. Aitken, Kenneth Brower, Frank Fraser Darling, Raymond Dasmann, John P. Milton, Noel Simon.

Publisher's note: This book is set in Centaur and Arrighi by Mackenzie & Harris, Inc., San Francisco. It was lithographed and bound by Arnoldo Mondadori Editore, Verona, on coated paper made by Cartiera Celdit and single-page collated and bound in Canapetta of C.I.A. Color separated by Gravure DeSchutter N.V., Antwerp. Design is by David Brower. Layout is by Amory Lovins.